# SHOW US THE STRAIGHT WAY

# Show Us the Straight Way

*The Intimate Act of Talking to God in Prayer*

Presenting the Wisdom of
Sufi Masters Seyyedeh Nahid Angha, Ph.D.
and Shah Nazar Seyyed Ali Kianfar, Ph.D.

Halima JoAnn Haymaker

International Association
of Sufism Publications

Copyright © 2019 Halima JoAnn Haymaker
ISBN # 978-0-9863592-8-6 (print)
ISBN # 978-0-9863592-9-3 (e-book)
Library of Congress Control Number: 2019919763
International Association of Sufism

All rights reserved. No part of this book may be reproduced or stored in a retrieval system, or transmitted in any forms or by any means, electronic or mechanical, including copying, recording or otherwise, without permission of the copyright owner.

This book does not imply any gender bias by the use of feminine or masculine terms, nouns or pronouns.

The International Association of Sufism is a publisher of many Sufi books and Sufi related materials. Books published by the IAS are the authors' views and the publisher takes no responsibility for any statement made by the authors in its publications.

For more information address the publisher:

International Association of Sufism
P.O. Box 2382
San Rafael, CA 94912
USA

Cover Design by Matthew Davis, Ph.D.

*All praise to Allah
The first and last
The beginning and the end
The Eternal Essence and
The Unity of all Being*

*Gratitude to
Uwaiysi Sufi Master
Hazrat Moulana Shah Maghsoud Sadegh Angha*

*Deepest appreciation and love to
Wise teachers and guides
Seyyedeh Nahid Angha and
Shah Nazar Seyyed Ali Kianfar*

*In the name of God, Most Gracious, Most Merciful.*
*Praise be to God, The Cherisher and Sustainer of the Worlds;*
*Most Gracious, Most Merciful;*
*Master of the Day of Judgment.*
*Thee do we worship and Thine aid we seek.*
***Show us the straight way**,*
*The way of those on whom Thou hast bestowed Thy Grace,*
*Those whose (portion) is not wrath, and who go not astray.*

Qur'an 1:1-7

# DEDICATION

To Hamid
My son
Who brought me to his teachers
To help me find the light

# TABLE OF CONTENTS

Introduction     xiii

### Part I: Prayers in Many Traditions

1. Have Human Beings Always Prayed?     3
2. What Is Prayer?     7
3. What Are Different Types of Prayer?     14
4. Why Do We Pray?     24
5. To Whom Do We Pray?     31
6. What Are the Results of Prayer?     40
7. What Have Scientific Studies Revealed about Prayer?     52
8. What Are Some Beautiful Prayers and *Zekr*?     57
9. How Do We Teach Children to Pray?     73

### Part II: Prayers in the Sufi Tradition

10. How Do Sufis Prepare to Pray?     81
11. What Is *Salat* – the Sufi Daily Prayer?     86

12. What Is the Sufi Prayer Called
    the *Fatiha*? 91
13. What Is *Zekr* – The Sufi Prayer of
    Remembrance? 98
14. What Is Sufi Meditation? 105
15. What Does the Qur'an Say about
    Prayer? 113

## Part III: Teachers of the Straight Way

16. What Is the Origin of Sufism? 121
17. Who Are Dr. Nahid Angha and
    Dr. Ali Kianfar? 128
18. What Is the International Association
    of Sufism? 137

Endnotes 143
Bibliography 155
Acknowledgements 167

# Introduction

The purpose of this book is to transmit the wisdom and guidance I have received over the past twenty-three years from my Sufi teachers, Seyyedeh Nahid Angha and Shah Nazar Seyyed Ali Kianfar. They taught me about God, far greater than I had ever imagined and much closer to me as well. When a previous image of God as a bearded white man no longer fit modern understanding, I began to examine my prayers. Was I still praying to that childhood vision of God? When I asked others to whom they pray, it became obvious there is a great deal of confusion. And so, this book began with the question: To whom am I praying? Other questions soon followed: Why do I pray at all? What is prayer, anyway? What happens when I pray?

I am grateful to my teachers, and to their teacher Hazrat Moulana Shah Maghsoud

Sadegh Angha, for bringing together modern scientific knowledge with ancient Sufi wisdom. In writing this book, I am attempting to distill into simple form their teachings about prayer along with some information and commentary about prayer from other scholars, spiritual and religious leaders and other faith traditions. By using the feminine pronoun throughout, I attempt to balance the use of the masculine pronoun during the past many centuries.

The title of the book, *Show Us the Straight Way,* is the sixth line of the Qur'an and part of the prayer that Sufis and all Muslims say five times a day. It reflects our heartfelt request for guidance. (For details on Sufism, the mystical path of Islam, see Chapter 16.)

Words translated into English from other languages, especially Hebrew and Arabic, are often spelled differently by different translators. Hence the same word may appear in various forms throughout the book and even, sometimes, on the same page.

All unattributed information and all wisdom in this book come from the oral teachings of my holy teachers, Dr. Angha and Dr. Kianfar. All quotations from the Holy Qur'an are from the 1987 version translated by Abdullah Yusuf Ali.

Any errors of fact and interpretation in this book are my own, and for them I apologize.

# Part I

Prayers in Many Traditions

# 1

# Have Human Beings Always Prayed?

Sufi Master Dr. Ali Kianfar says, "Searching for God is an innate drive in human beings."[1]

Who has not called out in time of fear or pain, "Help me, God"?

And who has not in time of great joy exclaimed, "Thank you, God"?

Or watching the suffering of another, who has not pleaded, "God, please help her"?

People of every race, nationality and religion, all over the world, are known to pray to a higher power by one of the various names for God – Allah, Ahura, Jehovah, Elohim, Yahweh, Adonai, Krishna, Vishnu. Dr. Larry Dossey says in his introduction to Thich Nhat Hanh's book, *The Energy of Prayer,* "We know of no cultures, past or present, in which prayer does not occur."[2]

As long as humans have existed, they have acknowledged an unseen power. Among the oldest records of human belief in a spiritual entity are prayers recorded in hieroglyphs as early as 2000 B.C.E. in Egypt.[3] Babylonian prayers to Ishtar from approximately 1600 B.C.E. have also been preserved.[4] And there are prayers in the Egyptian *Book of the Dead* from approximately 1250 B.C.E.[5]

Even some ancient prehistory markings, from before there was a written language in their culture, have mythic and religious significance attributed to them. The paintings in the Paleolithic caves at Lascaux in Southern France from c. 15,000 B.C.E. are believed to have had a spiritual purpose.[6] Also, the inscribed symbols on the Phaistos disc from the Minoan Palace on the island of Crete, c. 1850 B.C.E., have been interpreted by some, I was told on a visit there, as a hymn or prayer. In other parts of the world, prayers have been found in the oral tradition of the non-literate Algonkin Indian First People of North America.[7]

Timothy Verdon in *Art and Prayer* puts it this way, "To turn to God . . . is in fact natural for human beings, a spontaneous impulse in women and men of every culture and civilization in every historical period."[8] Philip and Carol Zaleski in *Prayer: A History* say, "The instinct for prayer and the sense of the divine arise simultaneously as immediate facts of consciousness. . . . This is a primordial and universal event in the history of human consciousness and the life of every human being."[9]

However, in the twentieth century, psychologist Sigmund Freud, himself a lifelong atheist, described the impulse to pray as a psychologically "neurotic practice."[10] Other scientific explanations have been offered by neurologists who have attributed the state of prayer to "a misfiring of neurons" in the brain.[11] And of course there are those who declare, following nineteenth century German philosopher Nietzsche, that God is dead. In the later twentieth century, after the Holocaust and Hiroshima, even *Time* magazine famously asked on an iconic 1966 cover, "Is God Dead?"

Nevertheless, a majority of the people in America in the twenty-first century still believe in God and still pray. In 2014, Pew research found that 63% of Americans believed in God. " More than half (55%) of Americans say they pray every day, according to a 2014 Pew Research Center survey, while 21% say they pray weekly or monthly."[12] Dr. Dossey in *Prayer Is Good Medicine* states that "over 90 percent of people pray."[13]

Dr. Kianfar teaches that spirituality is part of the "nature of the human being," as Dr. Amineh Pryor reports. "Longing for the divine is a sweet gift within the human being."[14] It is this gift of longing that continues to lead people to some form of prayer.

What, then, is this phenomenon we call prayer?

# 2

## What Is Prayer?

Dr. Kianfar says that the language of prayer is the longing of the heart.

Prayer may be the most authentic, intimate thing we do. When we pray, we are in touch with our most personal, heart-felt truth. We sometimes acknowledge things we have never before admitted to ourselves or said out loud or told to anyone.

Prayer may be described as a communication between ourselves and God. However, Dr. Kianfar says, "It is not the human being that initiates communication with God." According to the teachings of twentieth-century Sufi Master Moulana Shah Maghsoud, "It is not until God initiates that the student even begins to search for God."[1]

The communication, then, begins with the Source, is received by the human being, who then responds with something called prayer. In *The Illuminated Prayer*, Coleman Barks says that prayer is a tool to "nourish and strengthen" the human "longing to return to the Source."[2]

"Sufism teaches that every human being has a direct relationship with Divine."[3] Her prayer may consist of words, either spoken, sung or chanted; it may be silent; or it may be a wordless communication from the depth of one's being.

Many scholars and writers have described prayer in a variety of ways.

\* Donald Spoto says *In Silence: Why We Pray,* "Prayer may be spoken of as a profound sort of dialogue."[4]

\*Sherry Ruth Anderson and Patricia Hopkins in *The Feminine Face of God* have described prayer as "the cultivation and practice of inner attentiveness and receptivity, a special kind of listening, of 'tuning in.'" They also say, "prayer is communion with mystery."⁵

*In *Healing Words,* Dr. Dossey says, "Prayer may be a conscious activity, of course, but . . . it may flow also from the depths of the unconscious. Prayer may even emerge in dreams."⁶

*Benedictine Monk, Brother David Steindl-Rast suggests that genuine prayer often occurs in people "precisely at times when they are not saying prayers."⁷

*Richard Rohr of the Center for Action and Contemplation describes prayer in several ways. He says, "I use 'prayer' to mean *any interior journey or practice that allows you to experience faith, hope and love within yourself.*" He goes on, "The word 'prayer' has often been trivialized by making it merely into a way of asking for what you want or making announcements to God, as if God did not know. . . . It is not a technique for getting things, a pious exercise that somehow makes God happy, or a requirement for entry into heaven. Prayer is much more practicing heaven now." Also, "In prayer, we simply keep returning the divine gaze, and we become its reflection almost in spite of ourselves."[8]

In one of the most beautiful descriptions of prayer, Dr. Dossey says, prayer is "our tie to the absolute, a reminder of . . . that part of us that is infinite in space and time and is Divine."[9]

Most religious traditions have bodily movements connected with the act of prayer. In Judaism there is bowing and swaying. Christians are known to bow their heads in prayer, genuflect in church and kneel in the pew, at the altar, beside the bed, or on a *prie dieu*. Muslims have the traditional movements of the *salat* prayer that include both bowing and prostration.

Yet, it is not the formation of words or movements of the physical body that are the essential aspect of prayer. Rather it is a special quality of the heart that is necessary. Sufis teach that it is not prayer unless it comes from the heart. True prayer involves honesty, humility and also love.

When human beings experience events they do not understand, they seek to connect themselves to the source of the power that created those events. Dr. Kianfar teaches that "all forms of worship, regardless of the religious tradition, are designed to release oneself from limited authority and submit to or join, instead, to a greater authority and power."[10]

To ask for help is to admit one's limitation and with this comes humility. It involves the consciousness and acknowledgement that there is a greater or higher power who is in command of things beyond one's control.

Isaac of Syria, in the seventh century, said: "When someone is aware that he is in need of divine help, he makes many prayers. And once he has made much supplication, his heart is humbled, for there is no one who is in need and asks who is not humbled."[11]

Likewise, to stand in awe and wonder before the manifestation of the creative essence, a Mozart concerto or a field of spring wild flowers, or to be filled with joy at the sight of a newborn baby, is to open oneself to love. The next step is to understand, with humility, that we are surrounded by blessings in both our physical life and our spiritual life, not because we earned them nor because we deserve them, but by the grace and mercy of God, the Source of all things. This leads both to thanksgiving and to opening the heart in an outpouring of love. Dr. Kianfar says, "Praying is the movement of lovers."

Even beyond the words, movements, feelings of humility and love, there is in prayer the possibility of transcending the individual ego and reaching the experience of Unity with the Divine. This is the goal of Sufi prayer: closeness to God and ultimately oneness with the Essence of all things. Muslim scholar Seyyed Hossein Nasr says that in the highest form of prayer, "there is a complete integration of body, soul, and spirit in a consciousness that transcends the individual level."[12] Spoto says, "Authentic prayer . . . is about reaching within and beyond the imagined self to a greater purpose and power."[13] Barks says that in prayer, Sufis are "raising a mosque of indestructible light in the inner quarters of the heart."[14]

When a person experiences the transcendent wonder and power of prayer, praying may become a greater part of her life. She may soon learn that, as Dr. Kianfar says, every thought, word and action may be a prayer. This idea is also taught in the Christian tradition. "'All that a Christian does, even in eating and sleeping,' writes John Wesley in the eighteenth century, 'is prayer when it is done in simplicity according to the order of God.'"[15] Muslim scholar R. W. Maqsood puts it this way: "Prayer is any thought, word or action done with God in mind – and the true Muslim – who is aware of God constantly, really spends every waking moment . . . in a state of prayer."[16]

Theophan the Recluse, a 19th century Russian Orthodox priest said: "The primary thing is to stand before God and to go on standing before Him unceasingly, day and night, until the end of life."[17]

What, then, are these prayers that we say on different occasions?

# 3

# WHAT ARE DIFFERENT TYPES OF PRAYER?

Why is it that people have been intent on classifying prayer into types? The Catechism of the Catholic Church lists five types of prayer; the Episcopal Book of Common Prayer lists seven. The internet has entries for four, five, six and seven types of prayer. Writer Anne Lamott has addressed the types of prayers in her book, *Help, Thanks, Wow: The Three Essential Prayers*.

Without numbering them, the various classifications of prayer may include the following:

***Prayers of supplication**. This refers to requests, pleas and petitions or asking for help for oneself, perhaps the most frequent type of prayer.

In Sufism this category includes "*Dua*" or individual prayers in one's own language. This is a voluntary act "distinguished from the daily prayer *(salat)* which is required from all the faithful."[1]

In Christianity it includes what Catholics call the "Our Father" and Protestants, "The Lord's Prayer." Zen Buddhist priest Eko-Sana told me that prayers in his tradition are not for one person, but are inclusive for "all sentient beings," man and beast alike, excluding no one.

This type of prayer may also include confession, contrition and repentance as a precursor to asking. However, Timothy Verdon says, "The most natural form of prayer is the plea: the spontaneous cry for help that the creature raises to the creator."[2]

***Prayers of thanksgiving.**  These are prayers of gratitude and appreciation for what God has done or given. Grace before meals is one example. In her book, *Help, Thanks, Wow,* Anne

Lamott says several things about prayers of thanksgiving: "Gratitude begins in our hearts and then dovetails into behavior." and "Gratitude is peace." And also, "If we are lucky, gratitude becomes a habit."[3]

\***Prayers of worship.** These are prayers of adoration and awe. They express wonder and admiration for God. Included here are those prayers sometimes referred to as canonical, ritual or devotional prayers that have a set form and set wording, such as the Muslim *salat* which is always said in Arabic, the language in which it was received by the Prophet Mohammad (peace be upon him). These same prayers have been offered by millions of people for thousands of years. In canonical prayers "the individual worshipper conforms his or her particular soul to a form and reality that transcends the individual."[4]

These prayers often include statements of humility from the worshipper. Saint Teresa of Avila, a sixteenth century Carmelite nun, said, "the whole foundation of prayer must be laid in humility."[5]

\***Prayers of intercession.** These are prayers for the needs of others, sometimes called distant prayers. They may be prayers asking for healing or "directed prayer" asking for some definite outcome. Prayers asking for specific events tend to try "to structure the future, to 'tell God what to do,'" according to Dossey.[6] On the other hand, "nondirected prayer" asks only for the best outcome or the highest good.[7]

\***Prayers of remembrance.** In Sufism these prayers are often referred to as *zekr, zikr, dhikr*, among various spellings of the Arabic word translated into the English alphabet. Sufi Master Dr. Nahid Angha tells us that fifteen verses in the Qur'an command people to remember God.[8] The Prophet "advised his followers that the best of deeds is the *zekr* of the Lord."[9] These prayers often call on God by one of the "99 Beautiful Names." (See Chapter Twelve) Sufis sometimes use prayer beads, repeating a specific name over and over with each bead, as a practice of remembrance.

In other traditions prayers of remembrance may be called incantations, invocations or hymns.

\***Prayers of praise and love.** Sometimes called "prayers of the heart," this category includes the important Sufi practice of meditation. The Psalms of the Bible are also prayers of praise, and prayers of ecstasy may also be included here. Others refer to these prayers as contemplation or centering prayer.

Carol and Philip Zaleski say that "contemplation, unlike other forms of prayer . . . is a way of life." Contemplation is "like being in love. The borders of one's being melt; lover and beloved unite."[10]

Christian centering prayer is described as "learning to withdraw attention from our thoughts."[11] However, unlike Sufi meditation which strives for the experience of unity or oneness with the Divine, Christian centering prayer strives for "nondual consciousness . . . *as a mode of perception, not a state of mystical union.*"[12]

\***Prayers of Lamentation.** These are prayers of sorrow or grief for one who has died. This category includes requiems and elegies. Some beautiful and famous poems and music are in this form.

\***Listening as Prayer.** This is one of the ways that Mother Teresa defines prayer. It is also part of an "ancient Hebrew prayer (that) says, 'Sh'ma Yisraeil/ Hear O one who struggles with God/ listen O seeker of the way.'" And it is also the way of Christian monks in the Middle Ages, who practiced *lectio divina*, reading scripture and listening with the heart.[13]

\***Prayer Wheels.** The Tibetan prayer wheel is a special cylindrical wheel on a spindle with the purpose and intent of helping to relieve suffering in the world. Tibetan prayer wheels can be made of metal, wood, leather, stone or coarse fabric. Traditionally, the mantra *Om Mani Padme Hum* is written on the exterior of the canister in Sanskrit. This prayer cannot be translated into a simple phrase. Prayer wheels were in use as early as 400 C.E.

A Prayer wheel may be a single canister with a handle capable of being held and spun by an individual. Prayer wheels may also be groups of identical canisters ranging in size from a few inches to several feet tall. Inside the same mantra or others are inscribed on paper wrapped around a central core. "In some cases, thousands or even millions of prayers, mantras and good intentions can be wrapped around the center of the traditional prayer wheel." According to Tibetan Buddhist tradition, spinning a Tibetan prayer wheel can have the same positive effect as reading, reciting or meditating upon the mantras and prayers it contains.[14]

The Zaleskis describe homemade prayer wheels owned by a Tibetan friend. "One turned by hand, a second by wind, and a third – a particularly cunning device in the form of a lampshade – spun in convection currents emitted by the heat of a hundred-watt bulb. The Dalai Lama is on record as approving an even more technically advanced method for making a prayer wheel; download the *om mani padme hum* mantra to your computer's hard drive, where it will spin at a rate of some fifty-four hundred rotations per minute, calling forth the blessings . . . as effectively as do the older technologies of prayer."[15]

\***Unceasing Prayer.** Various traditions use the continuous repetition of a name of God or a phrase as a prayer. The unceasing Sufi *zekr or dhikr* may use the name "Allah" or one of various phrases. (See Chapter Seven) An example in Christianity is the Jesus Prayer.

\***Unconscious Prayer.** Dr. Dossey says, "If the urge toward oneness, unity and wholeness lies at the heart of prayer . . . we must consider seriously that prayer and dreaming are very closely related, and that we pray unconsciously night after night, dream after dream."[16]

\***Post-Modern Forms of Prayer.** There are forms of prayer that previous generations never heard of. These include what the Zaleskis call "self-healing prayer" and "self-help spirituality" including Dial-a-Prayer.[17] In Santa Rosa, California, "Drive Thru Prayer" is also offered.

Some prayers contain a combination of several types: the Jewish morning prayer is a "three-stage progression from praise and confession to petition to thanksgiving."[18]

Pamela Brode in *The Power of Prayer* says that the motions of praying mean nothing without love.[19] The Bible says, "If I speak in the tongues of men and angels, but have not love, I am become sounding brass, or a clanging cymbal." (I Corinthians 13:1, Revised Standard version)

Dr. Angha teaches that prayer must be offered without thought of reward. She says, "If an individual seeks a reward for his devotion, he is not pious but merely a business person. . . . Worship that is not inspired by the honesty of heart and ecstasy of life is either motivated by greed for the profits of the world or the desire for the blessings of Paradise."[20]

The essential thing that we are told in the holy books is that when we ask for help, God will answer. The Qur'an says, "Call on me; I will answer your (prayer)." (40:60) The Bible says, "Ask, and it shall be given you; seek, and ye shall find; knock, and it shall be opened unto you." (Matthew 7:7, King James version)

All of these varieties of prayer are available to us, but, really, why is it that we pray at all?

# 4

# Why Do We Pray?

*"There are times in the history of humanity when we may need more devotion, positive energy, active humanitarian participation, and prayers. This is one of those times."*
— Dr. Nahid Angha[1]

We are sometimes drawn to pray as a first response — to joy and happiness, and sometimes as a last resort — in pain and sorrow, when there is nothing else to turn to for help and comfort. We may pray for the survival of our planet. We may pray in the agony of remorse, asking for forgiveness. And sometimes there is an inner longing to understand who we are and where we came from that causes us to establish a communication with the Divine Source of All Being.

Dr. Angha describes the beginning of an individual's inquiry as the "recognition of the inadequacy of his own limited understanding and the desire to enlarge and ultimately transcend it." She says, "Ultimately, it is 'you' whom you are searching for . . .and the true essence of your being is the Divinity within you."[2]

In her book, *Principles of Sufism,* Dr. Angha says, "Worship that is based on traditional customs and empty imitation is bereft of truth . . . It is the heart of the believer that must become open to Being, so that it may see and hear truth until it can believe the reality of the Divine. . . . the *zekr* of God prepares the heart for such an opening."[3] (*Zekr* in Sufism refers to a prayer of remembrance.)

Many people come to prayer or contemplation from "great suffering or great love." Rohr says, "These are the quickest and most universal ways that God uses to destabilize the self-referential ego."[4]

In answer to the question, "Doesn't an omniscient God already know our most intimate needs and desires?" St. Augustine offers that "the purpose of prayer must be to transform the one who prays."[5]

A Sufi Sheikh who is a student of Dr. Kianfar's answered my question: Why do I pray? "I pray because I am trying to find my self. My essential, pure, original self. That self which is beyond the obscurations of personality and acquired identification. I have the idea that if I find my origin, I will also find myself there. My experience is that the movement of prayer is turning toward the light of awareness to find the source of awareness. I find this light within my own being, so turning toward means turning inward. This direction is found by recognition. Recognition is the echo of my own being within my own being, the resonance between the creator and the created which, when found are not two."

A Methodist minister described to me why she prays. "I feel the need to 'Lift to the Light,' as the Quakers say, what is on my heart:

gratitude, intercession—to open myself to honest perspective on my own life."

An Episcopal Deacon puts it this way: "I pray because I am not alone. I am connected to God. I live with God and need to be with God, spend time with God, ask for God's help, comment to God; and this is lived-out by talking with and being with God in prayer...verbal (spoken and unspoken) and non-verbal. In praying for other people or situations, I hold them (or the situation) in the Light of God... hold them together with God...hold them up to God's loving security, protection, and freedom. Except for the times when I am distracted, God's presence is inseparable from my consciousness."

A Zen Buddhist priest told me that in his tradition they pray to give homage to all Buddhas, past, present and future, for teachings, and for keeping alive for us the opportunity of enlightenment in this lifetime.

The authors of *The Feminine Face of God* say, "There is in us, it seems, some deep human need for connecting with truth. And the most direct and accessible way many of us make this connection is through prayer."[6]

Anne Lamott quotes author C. S. Lewis as saying, "I pray because I can't help myself. I pray because I'm helpless."[7]

According to the teachings of Dr. Angha and Dr. Kianfar there are many reasons why Sufis pray.

- We pray to open our heart.
- We pray to experience oneness with God and the unity of all things.
- We pray to discover truth.
- We pray to hold up a mirror to ourselves and see our own mistakes.
- We pray because saying the holy words and the names of God helps us in transformation.
- We pray to come close to God. This causes "Divine qualities [to] manifest in the worshiper."[8]
- We pray in order to become our best self.
- In *Principles of Sufism* Dr. Angha says, "The person who remembers Being and

always recollects himself will advance his knowledge on the path of understanding, and in so doing will learn to free himself from the leaden hand of ignorance."⁹

Sufi student Dr. Sarah Mullin reports on Dr. Kianfar's teaching about the prayer known as the *Fatiha* as follows. "As the practitioner prostrates in prayer, she acknowledges that everything she has received from God and all that she will receive will ultimately go back to God. She does not pray for any other reason than to increasingly submit to the energy of her Creator. Therefore, in Sufism, prayer is not ritual, and it is not for God (as the Divine is self-subsisting), and it is not because one is sinful (human beings are considered innately pure in Islam). It is only for the practitioner to become increasingly aligned with her divinity."¹⁰

Describing the teachings of Dr. Kianfar, Dr. Mullin says, "The practice of *Salat* describes both the Islamic prayer consisting of words and movement but more importantly describes a lifestyle of purity that the practitioner adopts.

Therefore, the practitioner who becomes more pure in her way of life ultimately lives in prayer."[11]

Let us close this chapter with the words of 11-12th century Sufi Sheikh Kazerouni who instructed, "Keep the *zekr* of the Almighty Lord in your heart, and keep the world in your hands; and never keep the *zekr* in your tongue and hold the world in your heart."[12]

Who is it exactly, then, that we pray to? Who is this "God"?

# 5

# To Whom Do We Pray?

Perhaps many of us no longer envision God as the elderly white man with a beard in the sky as portrayed by Michelangelo in the sixteenth century on the ceiling of the Sistine Chapel in Rome. If that is so, then to whom or what are we praying?

Hazrat Moulana Shah Maghsoud Sadegh Angha, twentieth century Uwaiysi Sufi Master, devoted his studies and teachings to integrating modern scientific thought with ancient Sufi wisdom. Hazrat Shah Maghsoud's daughter, Dr. Nahid Angha, has described what in Islam we refer to as "Allah." She says, "All the shapes, forms, colors, and energies in the universe are based on one thing, one essence.

Only one thing is the first and the last, the beginning and the end – this essence. We cannot really name it, but in Islam we call this essence 'Allah.' Each person is a manifestation of that essence. Our physical manifestation will fall away, but our base, our identity, our essence will remain. This is why we do not die. In our essence we are one with God. We are talking about one single thing – the essence, the unity of all being."[1]

Dr. Kianfar uses the words "Ultimate Reality" for the Divine essence. He tells us, we do not pray for God, we pray for ourselves. We pray to find our holy self. We are seeking to find ourselves in unity with Ultimate Reality, with the Divine. When we pray to the Divine essence, we pray to the whole, to the Unity of all Being, not to something separate from and outside ourselves. That is the meaning of one of the most common *zekr* in Islam and Sufism, *La illa ha illa Allah* (There is nothing except God). Therefore, we too contain the Divine essence within our heart. Praying can be a path to our inner being. In prayer our heart may experience unity with

Truth, with Reality. (See Chapter Thirteen for an explanation of *Zekr*.)

Dr. Kianfar explains, the *mind* is unable to understand Ultimate Reality. It is the wrong tool. It operates in the realm of the *external* environment. We use our senses to collect information to help us survive in our physical life. The mind stores these facts, but they are limited and in continual flux. The mind also contains memories and ideas from our parents and previous generations that are often harmful influences. We are seeking a deeper wisdom that is beyond the mind and the senses. It is in the spiritual heart that we can find knowledge of our inner self – that we can discover our innermost truth. It is there that we are connected with the essence of Being, with God.

True, innate divine knowledge is fixed, stable and unchanging. It is our original wisdom. It is the foundation of everything. We access this divine knowledge through the heart and through our praying and spiritual practice. The Prophet Mohammed (peace be upon him) instructed that praying should take place in the presence of the heart, otherwise it is not true praying. We need to leave our mind and move into our heart. It is said that we should enter our heart and lose our mind.

Dr. Kianfar says that when we see a tree, often we do not remember that its origin was in a seed. Our origin is also in a seed; not the physical seed of conception, but the Divine seed hidden in the heart. When we see a seed, we don't know what is contained within it. A seed, such as an acorn, contains an unseen, hidden potential, and so does the seed within our heart. The whole universe is wrapped within the seed. When we live only on the surface, in the physical world, we rarely remember our source in the seed, and we may never discover our true potential. There is an invisible energy within the seed, a deep wisdom. This is where we can access the self-knowledge we are seeking; this is the place where we find our connection with God.[2]

So, to whom do we pray? One answer is that we pray to the Divine seed within our heart. Ninth century Persian Sufi Master Al Hallaj said, "I saw my Lord with the Eye of the Heart. I said: 'Who art thou?' He answered 'Thou.'"[3]

The Qur'an says,

> "God is the Light of the heavens and the earth. The parable of His Light is as if there were a Niche and within it a Lamp: the Lamp enclosed in Glass: The Glass as it were a brilliant star: Lit from a blessed Tree, an Olive, neither of the East nor of the West, whose oil is well-nigh luminous, though fire scarce touched it; Light upon Light! God doth guide whom He will to His Light; God doth set forth Parables for men: and God doth know all things." (24:35)

This light is the light of wisdom, truth and love. Sufism teaches that in the heart of the human being is a mirror, and the Divine light constantly shines on that mirror. We can let that mirror become cloudy with our forgetfulness and ego-filled thoughts and actions. Or we can polish that mirror through prayer and meditation so that it becomes a clear mirror that reflects the Divine light, and we become a reflection of the one Divine light. Every single part of existence reflects only the one light.

(For details about Sufi prayer practice, see Part II – Prayers in the Sufi Tradition.)

My Sufi brother says, "I pray to the one who created me to guide me. It just seems inevitable to me that the way to my original self is illuminated by the one who created that self. In fact, it is my belief that there is no separation between the origin, the path, and the one who is created."

When I asked my very dear friend, Zen Buddhist Priest Eko-Sana, before he left his body, if Buddhists pray to the Buddha, he explained to me that perhaps that is so, but only in the sense that we are all Buddhas. They do not pray to some *one*.

My Presbyterian friend in South Carolina shared with me, "How and to whom one prays is a result of one's entire theology and understanding of God. I believe that God the Creator of all things is big, bigger than I can understand. I accept the mystery. My understanding is based on Jesus. But I also believe that God has revealed Himself through many other spiritual paths. So, I pray to God, through the revelation of Himself through Jesus and many others who followed in the Way. I have no picture of the physical 'God' – Michelangelo aside!

"My whole life is a prayer; I just ask God for help all during the day. I thank him many times a day for my life, my family and friends, this beautiful world – even for the pain that has taught me to trust in Him and others. And I pray for others, trying to forgive them as I ask for my own forgiveness. For me, it is anything but simple. It depends on my honesty with God and others – often hard."

Anderson and Hopkins say, "How we pray, the words we use to name that which we connect with – truth, God, the self, Great Spirit, or nature – do not matter. We sense intuitively when we are 'in communion' with our source, and it is then that we feel we are praying."[4]

Lamott calls this entity to which we pray "the Good, the force that is beyond our comprehension but that in our pain or supplication or relief we don't need to define."⁵

And yet, many people grew up with the concept of duality – God as separate from us and outside of us. So, when we say, "God, help me," we may fall back into the old pattern of asking for help from an outside source rather than looking for the light deep within to find the help we seek. Likewise, in Sufism, when we pray to the 99 Names of God, we may pray to "Ar-Rahim" – the Merciful, or to "Al-Ghaffar" – the Forgiver. For some it is easier to believe that the power lies outside ourselves and that someone else can help us or change things. The challenge is to find help, mercy and forgiveness by looking for the Source inside ourselves. This practice is much harder and requires a deep commitment. (See Chapter 13 for an explanation of the 99 Names of God.)

Dr. Kianfar states, "The 'God' who is now introduced and displayed by societies is not acceptable for seekers of truth. The substitution of a word for reality cannot satisfy. Finding an answer to the question of the reality of 'God' is the responsibility of every member of this great creation."

He goes on to say, "The Koran reads that, 'Religion is reality.' Thus, having religion is essentially discovering the reality of the 'self' for any human being. The knowledge of religion does not come by reading books, but in understanding the book of the self, from its most solid matter up to is most abstract form."

He explains further, "Sufism . . . concerns itself with the existence of God, His relationship with creation, and how each individual person can develop an understanding of divinity through observance and witnessing divinity. The message of the prophets is 'whoever knows oneself knows one's Lord.' It is up to each human being to discover his path to Divinity."[6]

Then, when we pray to the Divine Essence, the Unity of All Being, what are the results of this prayer?

# 6

# What Are the Results of Prayer?

While it is true that most people pray in times of crisis or of great joy, it is also true that many people question whether prayer "really works." "What *good* does it do to pray?" people often ask.

Katherine Preston describes Dr. Kianfar's teaching about the results of prayer as follows: "If I speak to God in a prayer in my own spoken language used in physical life, I may not get a response in spoken words. The response is not a language or a religion, it is a revelation of truth which is beyond time and space and the confines of ordinary language."[1]

The response to prayer or *zekr* may not come in words, but in an understanding of what is good or right behavior in answer to a question or petition. Dr. Kianfar says that when you pray correctly, you get the right response. It is like having a guitar tuned correctly.

There are others who suggest that the most dramatic and profound effect of prayer is on the one who is praying. Llewellyn Vaughn-Lee, twenty-first century Sufi teacher says, "As the heart's prayer deepens we merge more and more within the heart, into the oneness that is our divine promise. We step from the shores of our own aloneness, our sense of separation, into love's ocean where we are always with our Beloved."[2]

Amir-al-Moumenin Ali, the cousin and son-in-law of the Prophet, (peace be on them both) describes the results of *zekr* by saying it "enlightens the heart and pours forth blessings onto the *salek's* (student's) life."[3]

We are also taught that "The *zekr* of remembrance, when practiced properly, patiently and consistently, may wash judgment from our hearts and minds, (and) open our capacity for love and the recognition of beauty."[4]

In *The Nature of Miracle*, Dr. Angha describes the way in which prayer can affect energy in the universe. "When a group of people get together and form a circle of a united intention, their hearts connect and in this unified connection they begin to create an extremely powerful energy and electromagnetic system. In the union of energies, energies do not add, they multiply. And if there are extremely powerful people, with powerful concentration ability among this group, the multiplication of energy will increase even more. Such meditated and concentrated energy is creative and effective. It can create and it can direct to a favorable destination. It actually effects the course of energy waves."[5]

My Sufi friend explained to me:

"I find I have a lot of resistance to the word 'result,' perhaps because it seems to imply an attachment to outcome as the measure of the value of prayer. Yet, at the same time, I cannot deny that there have been many positive outcomes of prayer, both tangible and intangible. The question for me is where does one place one's priority? Is the ineffable less valuable than the clearly perceived? Who is the perceiver and what is the limitation of perception?

"In Islam, we refer to two names of God, *al-Zahir* and *al-Batin*, the Apparent and the Hidden. How these two aspects of the Divine manifest in a life and how they are interwoven is an unfolding story. It is the journey of spirituality. Prayer is the vehicle.

"For me, the deepest prayer is 'Thy will be done' in all its various expressions. It is relinquishing of attachment to outcome and an investment of trust in guidance of the one who created me. Islam is a variation on the Arabic word *taslim*, which means submission. 'Thy will be done' is an acknowledgment of the reality that we are already submitted. Knowing that we are already submitted means we are in the condition of receiving guidance. It is not a transaction. It is recognition.

"When the Bible says, 'Thy Will be done on earth as it is in heaven' it is an acknowledgment of the correspondence between the apparent and the hidden when one is in the condition of alignment with the Divine. As above, so below."

Dr. Kianfar adds: "The deepest prayer comes from the longing of the heart which never lies. It is beyond the control of the mind and the emotions, needs, or desires or expectations. It is the melody of love."[6]

Another friend, a Methodist minister, has this to say about the results of prayer. "My mother used to say there are no unanswered prayers, only different answers than we envision. Prayers of gratitude, thanks, fill me with openness to the beauty and goodness around me. These are specific prayers identifying all that is so much a part of my life, so I am filled by naming these moments, people, times. Prayers of intercession are also specific, putting the Bible and the newspaper together as one theologian put it. The world is so overwhelming in its need that I am lifted by sharing my pain at it all. Are those prayers answered? Often by empowering support for those who are trying to make a difference. And healing sometimes looks different than 'getting well.'

We are not relieved from the call to pray for all who hurt and those who hurt them just because we don't see immediate change. Sometimes prayer is what sustains us to keep at the tasks of peacemaking and healing."

An Episcopal Deacon describes the results of prayer in this way: "First of all, prayer can change me. It helps me to accept circumstances and people and put them all in a bigger picture than my little brain and ego-self by itself can understand. Secondly, the 'result' of praying for others or for circumstances and problems is that it helps them as well as us because it's done in love, for love, and in knowing that Love will reach them. If praying about evil, it brings God's power up against evil, and eventually love will win. This results in giving hope and confidence in times of trial, temptation, and pain. As Julian of Norwich said, 'All will be well, and all will be well, and all manner of thing will be well.'"

Anderson and Hopkins quote another woman who says, "In petitionary prayer, when we pray to God on behalf of another . . . people can feel and experience this good energy toward them. If all of us would only pray for each other it would be a very different world."[7]

Maya Angelou tells of her prayers for her paralyzed son and her faith that he would walk again. She says, "I *know* that prayer changes things. I know. I don't question. I know."[8]

Buddhist monk Thich Nhat Hahn says, "More than 200 controlled experiments in humans, plants, animals and even microbes suggest that the compassionate, loving prayers . . . of individuals can affect another individual or object at great distances." He also says, "When we send the energy of love and compassion to another person, it doesn't matter if they know we are sending it . . . that is truly prayer. In sending love outward, we may notice a change in our own heart."[9]

## Personal Accounts of the Results of Prayer

From a Presbyterian Deacon

*Jamie, my son, was born eight weeks early. He had a cleft lip. When he weighed almost ten pounds, I was able to take him back to Duke, where he was born, to have a cleft repair. I went alone because my husband was studying for the bar exam in Atlanta. I was twenty-four years old.*

*We were assigned to a double room in Duke Hospital. In the other bed was a beautiful four-year-old girl with lovely curls and bright eyes and a heart condition. Her mother was also there alone. Before they came to get our children, I bowed my head and said a short prayer sort of out loud.*

*I went to the cafeteria. When I came back to the room to wait for Jamie, I was shocked that the little girl's bed was empty, stripped, and her suitcase was gone. The nurse came in and told me she had died on the operating table.*

*God and I had a talk. For me, it forever changed my attitude toward prayer. I don't ask God for "results" that include specific outcomes anymore. I pray that I understand that God's time is not man's time and that by God's grace we are healed through faith, whether it is a lifelong belief or like the thief next to Jesus on the cross — at the last. It is always still amazing to me that I have faith that God wants a relationship with me and that prayer is the way I access that possibility.*

From a Sufi Sheikh

*In the time before I met my spiritual Teachers, I was in a feverish condition, figuratively and literally. I had been practicing meditation for some years and had been receiving instruction from someone who, though connected with Sufism was not affiliated with a tariqat (Sufi order) and did not claim to be a Teacher in the fullest sense. He was offering this as an introductory class but did not offer the opportunity to join a traditional path. As my experience of mediation was deepening, this became something of a conundrum, as I had the increasingly earnest desire to fully commit.*

*During this time, I had many experiences that, in hindsight, I realize predicted the path and Teachers I would find. But at that time, I could not see the way forward and, in this state, I developed a burning desire to find a Teacher. One of those experiences was the spontaneous, effortless memorization of the twenty-third Psalm, which eloquently speaks in the voice of one who is submitted to the Divine.*

*Over some months, the intensity of my longing increased, yet there was no evidence in the visible world of any opportunity to meet a teacher. As my desire became more ardent, the pain of my helplessness became agonizing.*

*This all culminated during a vacation over the Christmas holiday when I developed an abscessed tooth. The infection became so severe that I became feverish. It was quite intense, and later was told that I had become delirious but, in that state, I understood that it was a dangerous, potentially lethal, infection.*

*I began to spontaneously repeat the words "Thy will be done." I was not asking to be saved. I was simply acknowledging, quite deeply and sincerely, that I was in the hands of God. With each repetition, I experienced a deepening of my surrender. Finally, I let go completely into the state of acceptance. At that moment, my fever broke and I knew that I would be well.*

*Shortly after, when I returned to California, I was led to my Teachers. That is a story for another time, but at this moment I can say that they are Sufi Masters in an ancient lineage of which I'd never heard before, despite years of spiritual "seeking."*

*Was this the "result" of my praying? Or did God intervene? In my longing to know, I was led to guidance by guidance. So, did "I" pray or did God put that longing in me and draw me to Himself? In our tradition, it is said that Guidance is only by Allah. Rather than being the result of praying, perhaps praying is the result of Guidance.*

From a Sufi Sheikha

*When I was first diagnosed with cancer and we*

*did not yet know the extent or seriousness of it, the first response was shock. "What?" And as the reality set in, I began to consider just how I was going to cope with the treatments and, more significantly, with the approach of possible death.*

*I remember going into the spare bedroom, lying on the guest bed, and looking out the window at the trees and sky. I just began talking to God. "How am I going to deal with it if I am going to die?" I asked. Immediately I received an answer. "I will be with you always." My body did not die at that time, and that answer has carried me through the succeeding 30 years.*

So, you may ask, are there any scientific studies that demonstrate the results of prayer?

# 7

# WHAT HAVE SCIENTIFIC STUDIES REVEALED ABOUT PRAYER?

Larry Dossey, M.D., in two of his books, reports on the scientific studies that demonstrate the positive effects of prayer on health and healing in humans.

In *Prayer Is Good Medicine*, Dr. Dossey, says, "It is no longer a question of *whether* experiments prove that prayer works; *they have already done so.*"[1] Quoting David B. Larson, M.D. of the National Institute for Healthcare Research, he says, "If you go to church or pray regularly, it's very beneficial in terms of preventing illness, mental and physical, and you cope with illness much more effectively. If you look at the research, in area after area, it's 80 percent beneficial."[2]

In addition, Dr. Dossey says, "More than 130 controlled laboratory studies show, in general, that prayer or a prayerlike state of compassion, empathy, and love can bring about healthful changes in many types of living things, from humans to bacteria." And "more than 250 studies show that, on average, religious practice that includes prayer promotes health."[3]

In his book, *Healing Words: The Power of Prayer and the Practice of Medicine,* Dr. Dossey reports on two well-known studies of the effects of prayer. The Spindrift Studies in Salem, Oregon, involved "laboratory experiments showing that prayer works." Both directed prayer, asking for a specific outcome (cure his cancer), and non-directed prayer, with no specific outcome in mind (Thy will be done), were studied. Though there was proof that both methods were effective, "the non-directed technique appeared quantitatively more effective."[4]

Dr. Dossey reports, "In the experiments dealing with the effects of prayer in humans, researchers found that intercessory prayer was effective even when the recipient *did not know* he or she was being prayed for."[5]

The widely publicized studies at San Francisco General Hospital in the 1980s by cardiologist Randolph Byrd demonstrated the positive effects of prayer. In 2005 this study was "considered the most significant experiment to date in the scientific study of prayer," according to the Zaleskis. One group of 192 patients received daily prayer by Christians and another group of 201 patients received no prayer. This was a random, double-blind study in which "neither doctors nor patients knew which participants were receiving prayer." After ten months, when data was collected, results showed that "the prayed-over patients needed less antibiotic medication and fewer artificial breathing aids, suffered less pulmonary edema, and enjoyed a lower rate of death."[6] The initial conclusion was that prayer really worked, and newspapers around the world enthusiastically reported this finding.

Then the skeptics poured in with criticism of the study, and the Zaleskis end their discussion of this experiment with the observation: "One must conclude that Byrd's study was irredeemably flawed." They go on to say, "Compared to the Dossey's intoxicating zeal, the sober assessment of the skeptics is off-putting."[7] Dossey, however, reports that despite criticism of this study by other scientists, there was a dramatic effect in one clinical area (none of the prayed for patients needed intubation) and a 5 to 7 percent improvement in other areas over the control group. Ultimately Dr. Byrd concluded with these carefully chosen words: "these data 'suggest' that intercessory prayer has an effect in patients admitted to the coronary care unit."[8]

Dr. Dossey summarizes, "The *love* and *compassion* that one brings to prayer are extremely important. The scientific studies indicate that if these are not present, prayers have little or no effect." He adds, "Love, like hope, heals. It is the very foundation of prayer."[9]

The Zaleskis propose that perhaps the efficacy of prayer depends not on "an exchange between the creature and the Creator, but on 'some power inherent in prayer itself.'" They go on to say that we might "describe prayer as an undetected natural power akin to electromagnetism."[10]

What, then, are some of the prayers used by Sufis and by other faith traditions?

# 8

# What Are Some Beautiful Prayers and Zekr?

## Prayers From The Sufi Tradition

From *The Gratitude Prayer* by Hazrat Pir Moulana Shah Maghsoud Sedegh Angha, twentieth century Sufi Master, as presented by his wife Mah Talat Etemad Moghadam Angha in her book, *Al-Momenon: The Faithful*

In the Name of Allah, The Most High

An infinite praise, the eternal salute to the Essence of the One, Allah, the Eternal, the Absolute. He begetteth not, nor is he begotten. He, Who raised the heavens without pillars, spread out the skies and the earth and is firmly established on the Throne. He is the creator of water, lands and trees, the sun and the moon and the cycles of days and nights. He illuminated the heart of Tur Sina, the horizons of all manifestations and knows the essence of hearts. . . .

Allah, there is no god but He, the Living, the Self-Sustaining, the Eternal, Most Gracious, Most Merciful, Most Majestic, Most Bountiful. . . .

May the heart of the inner travelers be content, continuously. May Islam last eternally. May the sun of the seeker of heart remain illuminated. May the light of the Divine illuminate hearts.[1]

From *A Meditation: Payam-e-del* by Moulana Shah Maghsoud Sadegh Angha

You, the Protector, for the sake of my heart and before my breath stops in my chest and chokes in my throat – grant me my wish as you desire and increase the hope of my heart by Your bounty.

You, the Absolute Truth, before it is too late – descend beautifully and gracefully into my heart, the house of tranquility, and rejoice my waiting soul, for my time passes cruelly. . . .

You, the Protector of the trusting, the scattered flocks of my senses and intellect were under Your protection from the very time they were entrusted to the field of natural and physical life. . . . Now, as the energies of my youth lose their strength and my time runs short, and the footsteps of old age make their marks upon my face and body, do not leave me to myself! . . .

You, the most gracious One, do not leave me to myself, but forgive me out of Your greatness and touch me with Your presence.[2]

*New Year's Prayer* by Seyyedeh Hamaseh Angha Kianfar, twenty-first century Sufi teacher, granddaughter of Moulana Shah Maghsoud, on 3/20/01

In the Name of Allah the most gracious the most merciful.
Oh, Allah, please make us worthy of being your servants.
Please guide us on the straight path and continue
To teach us the meaning of service and humility.
Give us eyes that see and ears that hear.
Please continue to help our Sufi community grow
And develop strong attachments with one another.
*Rabbenah Ottena Fedonya Hasane va fel akherate Hasane vagena azabenar.*[3]

From Ibn' Arabi, 12th century Sufi

Enter me, O Lord, into the deep of the Ocean of Thine Infinite Oneness.[4]

## Prayers From The Jewish Tradition

The *Shema*

*Shema Yisrael* "Hear, [O] Israel" are the first two words of a section of the Torah, and is the title of a prayer that serves as a centerpiece of the morning and evening Jewish prayer services.

*She-ma yisrael, adonai eloheinu, adonai echad*

Hear O' Israel, the Lord is our God, the Lord is One. (Deuteronomy 6:4)

This is recited at the climactic moment of the final prayer of Yom Kippur, the holiest day of the year, and traditionally as the last words before death.

The remainder of the *Shema* prayer is taken from three biblical sources: Deuteronomy 6:5-9; 11:13-21; and Numbers 15:37-41.[5]

## Prayers From The Torah And Bible

From *The Old Testament of the Bible*
*Psalm 23*

The LORD *is* my shepherd; I shall not want.

He maketh me to lie down in green pastures: he leadeth me beside the still waters.

He restoreth my soul: he leadeth me in the paths of righteousness for his name's sake.

Yea, though I walk through the valley of the shadow of death, I will fear no evil: for thou *art* with me; thy rod and thy staff they comfort me.

Thou preparest a table before me in the presence of mine enemies: thou anointest my head with oil; my cup runneth over.

Surely goodness and mercy shall follow me all the days of my life: and I will dwell in the house of the LORD for ever.[6]

From *The New Testament of the Bible*
*The Lord's Prayer* or the *"Our Father"*

Our Father, which art in heaven,
Hallowed be thy name.
Thy kingdom come; thy will be done
In earth, as *it is* in heaven.
Give us this day our daily bread.
And forgive us our debts,
As we forgive our debtors.

And lead us not into temptation;
But deliver us from evil:
For thine is the kingdom, and the power,
And the glory, for ever. Amen.[7]

## PRAYERS FROM THE CATHOLIC TRADITION

*The Hail Mary*

Hail Mary, full of grace. The Lord is with thee.
Blessed art thou amongst women,
and blessed is the fruit of thy womb, Jesus.
Holy Mary, Mother of God,
pray for us sinners,
now and at the hour of our death. Amen.[8]

## PRAYERS FROM THE EPISCOPAL TRADITION

From *"Compline"* in the *Book of Common Prayer*

"Keep watch, dear Lord, with those who work, or watch, or weep this night, and give your angels charge over those who sleep. Tend the sick, Lord Christ; give rest to the weary, bless the dying, soothe the suffering, pity the afflicted, shield the joyous; and all for your love's sake."[9]

*From the Book of Common Prayer*

O God, you made us in your own image and redeemed us through Jesus your Son: Look with compassion on the whole human family; take away the arrogance and hatred which infect our hearts; break down the walls that separate us; unite us in bonds of love; and work through our struggle and confusion to accomplish your purposes on earth; that, in your good time, all nations and races may serve you in harmony around your heavenly throne; through Jesus Christ our Lord. Amen.[10]

## OTHER CHRISTIAN PRAYERS

*The Jesus Prayer*

Lord Jesus Christ, have mercy on me.

The Jesus Prayer has become, after the Lords'

Prayer and the Hail Mary, perhaps the most popular Christian prayer. It is based on its continuous repetition. Various physical postures are often used during this prayer. The Zaleskis say, "the use of a prayer rope – a cord with one hundred evenly spaced knots – is nearly de rigueur, to keep count and to stabilize the mind."[11]

*The Serenity Prayer*

God grant us the serenity to accept the things we cannot change, courage to change the things we can, and wisdom to know the difference.[12]

*The Peace Prayer of Saint Francis*

Lord, make me an instrument of your peace:
    where there is hatred, let me sow love;
    where there is injury, pardon;
    where there is doubt, faith;
    where there is despair, hope;
    where there is darkness, light;
    where there is sadness, joy.

O divine Master, grant that I may not so much seek
   to be consoled as to console,
   to be understood as to understand,
   to be loved as to love.
   For it is in giving that we receive,
   it is in pardoning that we are pardoned,
   and it is in dying that we are born to eternal life.
   Amen.[13]

## Prayers From The Zen Buddhist Tradition

Courtesy of manuscript from the Sonoma Mountain Zen Center

*Maha Prajna Paramita Heart Sutra*

Avalokiteshvara Bodhisattva practicing deep Prajna Paramita
   Clearly saw that all five conditions are empty
   Thus was relieved from all suffering and fear.

O Shariputra, form is no other than emptiness, emptiness no other than form:

Sensation, perception, discrimination, consciousness, are likewise like this.

O Shariputra, all dharmas are forms of emptiness, not born, not destroyed, not tainted, not pure, without gain, without loss;

So in emptiness, there is not form, no sensation, perception, discrimination, consciousness;

No eye, ear, nose, tongue, body, mind; No color, sound, smell, taste, touch, phenomena, No realm of sight and so forth until no realm of consciousness,

No ignorance, and no extinction of it, and so forth until no old age and death and extinction of them; No suffering, no cause of suffering, no extinguishing, no path, no wisdom and no gain.

With nothing to attain, the Bodhisattva lives Prajna Paramita,

With no hindrance in the mind, there is no hindrance, therefore no fear exists:

Far beyond deluded thoughts, this is Nirvana.

All past, present, and future Buddhas live Prajna Paramita, and therefore, attain Anuttrara Samyak Sambodhi!

Therefore know, Prajna Paramita is the great mantra, is the great bright mantra, is the supreme mantra, is the unsurpassable mantra.

It is capable of relieving all suffering. This is true, not false. So proclaim the Prajna Paramita Mantra, Proclaim this mantra, and say: Gate! Gate! Paragate! Parasamgate! Bodhi! Savha!

## Prayers From The Buddhist Tradition

### A BUDDHIST FORM OF PRAYER
From my friend Susan

I have had a Buddhist meditation practice for many years, and I'm drawn to the *Brahma-viharas*, also known as the Four Immeasurables. The *Brahma-viharas* are a set of four Buddhist virtues and the practices used to cultivate them, thus bringing them into daily life as heartfelt and habitual responses. The four virtues are compassion, loving kindness, empathetic joy (delight in another's good fortune), and equanimity.

A practice for cultivating loving kindness known as *Metta* is my way of praying. *Metta* is first done for oneself, and then, if desired, for another, or a group of beings. I sit with my eyes closed, centered on my breathing, as I begin. The words can be personalized and expanded upon as you see fit.

## METTA PRACTICE

may I be safe and free from danger, from fear and anxiety. may I be safe.

may I be happy. may I be grateful for the gifts and the benefits in my life. may I cultivate a thankful heart.

may I be well, in body and mind and heart and spirit. may I be well.

may I live my life with ease, and courage, fortitude, love, wisdom, acceptance and gratitude. may I live my life with ease.

may all beings realize the light of their own

true nature. may all beings live with peace and well-being. may all beings be free.

## Prayers From The Hindu Tradition

From *"Songs from Prison"* by Mahatma Gandhi

"Grant me, O Master, by thy grace
To follow all the good and pure,
To be content with simple things;
To use my fellows not as means but ends
To serve them stalwartly, in thought, word, deed;
Never to utter word of hatred or of shame:
To cast away all selfishness and pride:
To speak no ill of others:
To have a mind at peace,
Set free from care, and led astray from thee
Neither by happiness nor woe;
Set thou my feet upon this path,
And keep me steadfast in it,
Thus only shall I please thee, serve thee right."[14]

From *Gitanjali* by Rabindranath Tagore, early twentieth-century Nobel Prize winning poet

"This is my prayer to thee, my lord – strike, strike at the root of penury in my heart.
Give me the strength lightly to bear my joys and sorrows.
Give me the strength to make my love fruitful in service.
Give me the strength never to disown the poor or bend my knees before insolent might.
Give me the strength to raise my mind high above daily trifles.
And give me the strength to surrender my strength to thy will with love."[15]

## SOME BEAUTIFUL *ZEKR*

The *Zekr* are spoken, chanted or sung in Arabic. The English translation is included below each *Zekr*. (See Chapter 13 for details on Zekr)

*Alhamdulallah*
All praises to Allah (God)

*Allah'hu Ackbar*
Allah (God) is the Greatest

*Shukran Allah*
Thanks be to Allah (God)

*La illa ha illa Allah*
There is nothing but Allah (God)

*Ya Allah, Ya Alim, Ya Rahman, Ya Rahim*
I call upon Allah (God), the All-Knowing, the Most Gracious, the Most Merciful
(These are among the 99 Beautiful Names of Allah. See Chapter 13)

*Ya Ali*
I call upon the Most High

These are the words, but how do we actually learn to pray?

# 9

# How Do We Teach Children to Pray?

Some of us pray because we were taught to pray as very young children by our parents or grandparents, and we have prayed our whole life. Some children remember first observing someone at prayer when they saw a family member praying either at home, mosque or *khanaghah* (Sufi prayer center), church or synagogue. This speaks to the significance of the parent or grandparent praying and allowing the child to witness him or her at prayer. The child may also observe, early in her life, the Sufi Master, minister, priest or rabbi leading a prayer. Therefore, it is also important to take the young child to the place of worship where she can see others at prayer, even if it is for a brief period of time. It is most important, however, that children are introduced to an unseen, inner world. They may be taught about a loving God, the creator of all life, who can be found within their heart.

Often the child's first act of prayer is an imitation of the adult's physical movements of the Muslim prayer or the kneeling or bowed head of the Christian. In Sufism children are often taught the simple *zekr* of "Allah" as their first verbal prayer. Later they may learn the phrase "*La illa ha illa Allah*" (There is nothing but God) as their first words in Arabic. To learn, first the *Fatiha* (first seven verses of the Qur'an), and later the entire daily prayer in Arabic, they are often taught one line at a time. In Christian Sunday School children are often taught the Lord's Prayer in the same manner.

Children may also be taught to pray

- when there is a death of a family member

or friend as a means of providing them with comfort and understanding
- when someone close to them is ill
- when they are afraid
- when they are embarking on a new or difficult endeavor
- when they are feeling thankful and happy

Some children simply go through the motions of prayer because it is expected of them, but without heart connection. This may allow them to have true prayer open to them as an option when they are ready to embrace it. Other children talk to God in all innocence from an early age.

Mysticism (belief in the ability to have direct communion with God, with the unseen) is easy for young children to understand because they frequently inhabit a world of the unseen. They may have invisible playmates or converse with spirit animals. Listening to the child and taking this seriously is important as an avenue to teaching her about God. A child who spends time outdoors may also understand the concept of the unity of all life.

In the past, the most common prayer that children in the Christian tradition have been taught is the following from eighteenth century England:

*Now I lay me down to sleep, I pray the Lord my soul to keep. If I should die before I wake, I pray the Lord my soul to take.*

In modern times a happier version substitutes one of the following second sentences:

*Keep me safely through the night and wake me at the morning light.*

*Guard me while I sleep tonight and wake me safe at dawn's first light.*

True prayer is a voluntary act to which some children are drawn. The Qur'an says,

*"Let there be no compulsion in religion: Truth stands out clear from Error: whoever rejects Evil and believes in God hath grasped the most trustworthy hand-hold, that never breaks."* (2:256)

It is important to listen to the child and to her prayers to understand the child's inner heart and to help with her spiritual development. The child may experience confidence and faith when she first learns to grasp that handhold and this faith may last throughout her life.

Is there any preparation required before we begin our prayer?

# Part II

Prayers in the Sufi Tradition

# 10

## How Do Sufis Prepare to Pray?

In his book *The Zekr,* as well as in his oral teachings, Dr. Kianfar describes the way Sufis are to prepare for prayer:

1. **Cleanliness**. "Cleanliness refers to both apparent and inner cleaning and purity. The body and the clothing of the performer of prayer must be clean."[1] Of course, the place for prayer must be kept scrupulously clean, and students are instructed to wear clean, white clothing used only for prayer. Inward purification is required to "purify one's heart from

the earthly attachments and set oneself free from everything except God."[2]
2. **Clothing**. As well as clean garments, Sufi Master Moulana Shah Maghsoud says that a person performing prayer must also wear "the clothing of piety, honesty, repentance and sincerity inwardly."[3]
3. **Place**. Sufis use a praying rug for their prayer at a private place in their home. Dr. Kianfar relates that "the Prophet Mohammad says that prayer is not a prayer unless it is performed at the presence of heart."[4]
4. **Direction**. The direction for praying is toward the Kabaa in Mecca. "The Moslems from all over the world perform prayer toward the same direction."[5]
5. **Time.** Sufis, like all Muslims, pray five times each day. "Prayers are said at dawn, noon, mid-afternoon, sunset and nightfall, and thus determine the rhythm of the entire day."[6]

> The Kabaa is a huge cube made of granite blocks built on a site sacred since ancient times. Today it is covered with a black cloth embroidered with golden calligraphy. The Kabaa is encircled by the Sacred Mosque with its two minarets. The Prophet Mohammad dedicated this ancient shrine to Allah in 632 C.E. and later commanded in the Qur'an, "Turn then thy face in the direction of the sacred Mosque; wherever ye are." (2:144)

6. **Washing.** "Before performing any prayer one must perform ablution as it has been instructed in the Koran V:6. 'Ye who believe when ye prepare for prayer wash your face, and your hands to the elbows, wipe your head with your hand from back to front and wash your feet to the ankle.'"[7]

Instructions from Dr. Kianfar for saying your prayers:

1. Make praying your first priority. Praying is a service to yourself.
2. It is a great honor to sit on your praying rug and talk to the Divine Source. You are sitting in the presence of God when you sit on your prayer rug. Pray from love, not asking for anything.
3. It is important that you hold your intention to connect with the Divine.
4. When you pray, you are seeking to establish a personal relationship between yourself and God.
5. You must let go of your ego and personality and move into your heart.
6. While you pray, make a straight line from your heart to God.
7. If praying is hard for you, your system is out of alignment. Do not pray when you are out of balance. Let the storm pass, find peace, then pray.
8. During your prayers, do not put God on hold while you think of something else.
9. When you pray sincerely, God leads the prayer.

When you are ready to pray, Dr. Kianfar gives three instructions:

1. Take a deep breath, hold it, then exhale the darkness from your system. Repeat this practice five times.
2. Stand beside your praying rug and wait for permission to pray. Be clear on your intention to pray.
3. Do not begin to pray until you are called by God.

Dr. Kianfar also teaches that "the individual who performs prayer [must] be aware that the intention is to get close to God. He is to follow this intention throughout the prayer. . . . He must become absent from himself and present in his heart. . . . Closeness to God is achieved only when all the thoughts and imagination of 'self' are eliminated."[8]

What is the special prayer that Sufis and all Muslims offer five times a day?

# 11

# What Is Salat – the Sufi Daily Prayer?

One of the many beauties of Sufism is the five times a day prayer, the *Salat,* which Sufis, like all Muslims, perform at specified times. In performing this prayer, "roughly one quarter of the earth's population prostrates itself toward Mecca."[1] This is "the greatest single act of devotion in all of human history."[2]

This prayer enables believers to pause from their mundane, worldly activities during the day and evening and address their "most gracious, most merciful" God in praise and thanksgiving. "The intention of *salat* is to become close to God . . . to return to our origin according to the principle of Unity."³

Dr. Nasr states that each person "stands directly before God in the daily prayers without any intermediary." He goes on to say that we are created so that we are able to address God "with free will." He explains that "The raison d'etre of being human . . . is to worship God and seek his help."⁴

The prayer is offered in Arabic, the language of the Qur'an. Although all five prayers begin with the first seven lines of The Qur'an, known as the *Fatiha,* they are not all alike. The morning prayer is the shortest with two rounds or stanzas, the sunset prayer has three rounds, and the other three are identical with four rounds each. A detailed description of the prayer is provided by Dr. Kianfar in his book, *The Zekr.* The Arabic and the English translation of the *Fatiha* may be found in Chapter Twelve.

There are five prescribed bodily movements that accompany the prayer, including bowing and prostrating with the forehead to the floor. Dr. Kianfar says, "The agreement between mind, heart and apparent movements show the strength, immensity, and the perfection of the prayer." He goes on to discuss his teacher's contribution to the understanding of the movements. "The first man in the history of Islamic Sufism to announce the secret of these movements was *Hazrat* Shah Maghsoud. In his lectures and books he revealed the secrets of these movements, teaching that the combination of the five necessary movements form the holy verse of La illaha illah-lah." (There is nothing but God).[5] In other words, "When carefully studying the physical movements, the body actually 'writes' '*La illa ha illa Allah*' as it moves."[6]

In reporting on Dr. Kianfar's teachings, Sherri Brown says, "When we are in prostration on the earth:

- Our head is in complete submission...
- Our two hands are open for the action of service for all beings and service to the earth
- Our two knees represent stability
- Our two feet walk in service and action.

This demonstrates a complete awareness and acknowledgement of all that we receive, the gratitude we have for our life, and our opportunity to return service to the earth."[7]

Dr. Nasr asserts that the form of the complete prayer "has descended from Heaven" and "the movements of the body and what the tongue recites (always in Arabic) were revealed to the Prophet by God, according to Islamic belief; they are not man made."[8]

Sufis sometimes say the words slowly, clearly becoming aware of the meaning of each word being said in Arabic. Sometimes the believer will say the words at a more rapid pace and let the beauty and power of the Arabic pour over her. Sometimes, a petitioner may strive to say the first stanza in a single breath.

Coleman Barks says, "There is no single word in English that conveys the scope of the Arabic word *Salat*." All words "fail to convey the Salat's marvelous integration of devotional heart surrender with physical motion. In Salat, our entire being is engaged in a single luminous event."[9]

Since Dr. Kianfar has explained that prayer must be performed in the presence of the heart, the challenge for the Sufi, and perhaps for all worshipers, is to find the way to open the heart, move into the heart and speak her deepest truth, with or without words. To find this authentic self is to let go of our ego, our personality, the external construct of who we are. We are taught to submit our entire being to the Source, the Absolute, the Eternal. This is the practice of Sufism, the straight way that we strive to follow.

Now, let's examine the *Fatiha*, the beginning of the Sufi prayer.

# 12

# What Is the Sufi Prayer Called the Fatiha?

The *Fatiha* is the first chapter of the Qur'an consisting of seven lines. It is the beginning of each of the daily Muslim prayers. It is always said in Arabic, the language of the Qur'an.

Dr. Kianfar teaches that the Arabic language which we find written down is not the language in which God spoke to the Prophet. It is a translation of the first language. The first language is the language of the Divine. This is not the language of the mind; it is the language of the heart. Words alone are not capable of translating the meaning. We learn the true meaning of the *Fatiha* through our heart by practice and experience.

Below is a guide to the Arabic pronunciation of the *Fatiha*.

*Bismillaah ar-Rahman ar-Raheem*
*Al hamdu lillaahi rabbil 'alameen*
*Ar-Rahman ar-Raheem Maaliki yaumid Deen*
*Iyyaaka na'abudu wa iyyaaka nasta'een*
*Ihdinas siraatal mustaqeem*
*Siraatal ladheena an 'amta' alaihim*
*Ghairil maghduubi' alaihim waladaaleen*[1]

The *Fatiha* is translated into English below.

*In the name of God, the Most Gracious and most Merciful*
*(Praise be to God) the Cherisher and Sustainer of the Worlds*
*Most Gracious, Most Merciful. Master of the Day of Judgment.*
*Thee do we worship and Thine aid we seek.*
*Show us the straight way,*

*The way of those on whom Thou hast bestowed Thy Grace;*
*Those whose (portion) is not wrath, and who go not astray.*²

The *Fatiha*, at the opening of the Qur'an, introduces a loving God who gives all people directions on how to live the life of good and faithful servants and receive divine blessings. Dr. Nasr says that the *Fatiha* "is the heart of the Qur'an and contains the message pertaining to the dimensions of the ultimate relation between human beings and God."³

In line one we learn that Allah is a loving and forgiving God. Line two tells us that Allah is a caring and protective God as long as we listen to him, and line three indicates that God will lead us to justice and balance and to the divine light. In line four we are taught that through prayer we can open ourselves to receive light and truth. The straight way is the path of Sufism, the journey toward purification of the heart and the search for knowledge. Frithjof Schuon says

"It is through Grace alone that we can follow this path; but we must open ourselves to that Grace."[4] Finally, we are guided on the path by our teachers who have found the light, and we seek a path of peacefulness.

Dr. Kianfar states that the *Fatiha* provides a guide for practice on our spiritual journey. The following summaries are based on Dr. Mullin's accounts of Dr. Kianfar's teachings in her book, *The Book of Self*. The prayer begins by naming God, the basis for all of our belief and actions. God is not a being, but a metaphor describing the entirety of existence. We learn that in praising him we accept and appreciate that all we experience is because of God. Then, following the teacher's instructions for meditation, we have the potential to experience the divine light. We are told to practice until we find the straight line to God. Finally, there is an emphasis on the need for balance and stability as the student maintains her spiritual intention.[5]

Dr. Kianfar teaches that another way to understand the *Fatiha* is to read it from bottom to top, starting with line seven. This study will help us perfect ourselves in the seven stages of the spiritual journey. In the first stage, the seeker concentrates on purifying herself so that she no longer associates with what distracts her from her goal. In the second stage she strengthens her intention to look for guidance from the Divine instead of following her own wishes.

In the third stage, she chooses where to apply her energy and takes part in daily activities that benefit her spiritual journey. Patience is an important characteristic in the fourth stage so that she may remain stable in her quest for spiritual experience.

In the fifth stage of spiritual development the seeker strives to constantly remain in prayer and live a pure life. The practitioner in the sixth stage is now in love with the process of attaining self-knowledge.

Finally, in the seventh stage of spiritual development, the seeker "ultimately confesses his nothingness and exchanges attachment to his ego for the identity of the Divine. . . . One who has perfected each of the seven stages of development has reached the highest level of spiritual understanding, transforming his entire way of life to reflect the divine essence."[6]

We turn to the Holy Qur'an as a guide to wisdom and knowledge, and in its first lines, the *Fatiha* provides the direction for our spiritual journey.

Islamic Scholar Annemarie Schimmel says, "Whoever has studied the Koran admits that reading and reciting it is a veritable conversation with God, who can be approached only through His word. Therefore, one would be justified in calling the reading of the Koran a 'sacrament.'"[7]

In closing this chapter, I offer my own inner thoughts and understanding as I say this beautiful prayer many times each day.

*Everything I do, I do as a servant of Allah, the One and Only.*

*Allah accepts me because of Grace, not because I deserve it.*

*God loves me and all of her creation and there will be no end to her creation.*

*Through her Grace she teaches me and through*

*her Mercy I have been granted the potential to learn.*

*Her creation is based on truth, balance and justice.*

*Allah is the only one I worship, and she is my only source of help.*

*If I ask with clear intention and a pure heart, she will show me the way to live an honorable life and the way to be directly in contact with her in this life and always.*

*My Holy Teachers who have found the light of Allah are the ones who will guide me and teach me how to find the straight path to God.*

*To avoid losing my way, making mistakes and doing wrong, I need to avoid those people and those parts of me that have turned away from God and her path of righteousness. Amen.*

Another important Sufi practice is *zekr*. What is the *zekr* prayer?

# 13

# What Is Zekr – The Sufi Prayer of Remembrance?

The word "*zekr*," sometimes spelled *zikr*, or *dhikr*, refers to a type of Sufi prayer. Sometimes *zekr* indicates the repetition of a single word, "Allah" or one of the "99 Beautiful Names of Allah" such a "*As Salam*" (The source of Peace.) *Zekr* may also signify a sentence or phrase, most commonly, "*La Illa ha Illa Allah*" (There is nothing but God), which Moulana Shah Maghsoud says is the highest *zekr*. *Zekr* may even mean the entire *salat*, the daily prayer.[1]

## The 99 Beautiful Names of Allah

The ninety-nine Beautiful Names of God are found in the Qur'an. The names represent the character traits of the Divine.

"The Names are the doors to understanding. Remembering and repeating the Names is a distinct form of worship and a sign of wisdom."[2]

*"Say: Call upon God or call upon Rahman: By whatever name ye call upon Him, (it is well) For to Him belong the Most Beautiful Names."* Qur'an, 17:110

See Illumination of the Names with an introduction from the teachings of Shah Nazar Seyyed Ali Kianfar.

The teacher may instruct the Sufi student to use a particular *zekr* in her private, personal prayer, performed in solitude. Or the teacher may lead a *zekr* for a group of students at a

Sufi gathering. There are occasions when several Sufi orders come together for a large group *zekr*.

The *zekr* may be said silently, aloud, sung – sometimes with instrumental accompaniment – or chanted in a rhythmical manner.

*Zekr* is an Arabic word that may be translated as "remembrance." What is it that students are called to remember? On the simplest level, it is the remembrance of God. On a deeper level, however, it is a remembrance of the Rule of Unity, the basis of Islam and Sufism. It begins with the belief in one God (*La illa ha illa Allah* – There is nothing but God). But it extends further to the understanding that in our pure center, we are part of the Divine Essence. And all beings, at their true core, also contain this Essence. So, we are all part of the Essence, and there is only One Essence: Unity.

Dr. Kianfar tells us, this "practice does not involve remembering with the mind."[3] Students are told that no prayer is acceptable unless it is from the domain of the heart. "Even praying can become an obsession if praying is from the domain of the mind. Praying from the mind is a much different stance and will bring a different outcome than seeking understanding and the experience of la illa ha illa Allah."[4]

This remembrance is mystical, beyond words, and touches our inner being. Especially in the form of chant, and particularly in a group of like-minded people, it may lead to a profound spiritual opening, including true ecstasy, the experience of leaving of the body. It also leaves one filled with love and often overcome with emotion. In Sufism this state is often referred to as drunkenness, a confusing term to some, since Sufis, like all Muslims, refrain from the use of alcohol. Dr. Kianfar explains, "The repetition of a holy name activates that which is wrapped within us."[5]

One does not begin a *zekr*, alone or in a group, without proper preparation. As with the daily prayer, *salat*, a student must begin with purification. This refers not only to cleanliness, clothing, and other things mentioned in Chapter Ten, but to purification of the heart. Purification in Sufism involves becoming a sculptor and chipping away all of the stone that is not the pure "me" to find the work of art that is the true essence of our being. It is sometimes spoken of as "letting go of all that is not me." Purification in Sufism in no way refers to purification from sin, since Sufis believe that human beings are born pure, not in sin. Dr. Kianfar says that the *zekr* will purify your whole system, much like sterilizing a jar for canning.

Next the student must have a clear focus on her goal. She must understand what it is that she is looking for and what she intends to accomplish. Students of Sufism are often told to "clarify your intention." Dr. Kianfar instructs, "To perform zikr properly requires perfect and pure intention and a clear focus, without distraction."[6] Students are encouraged to bring all their attention and energy to their heart and maintain that focus during the *zekr*.

Frequently, after preparation of the student, the teacher will "provide a holy name along with instructions for how to activate it. This practice often involves a certain number of repetitions done in a specific manner, at a specific time and place, and for a specific number of days. . . . The zikr then elevates us to the station where we can receive."[7]

Dr. Angha explains that there are many *zekr*. "The *zekr* of the tongue is the verbal *zekr*. It is practiced through the repetition of a phrase or a word as instructed by the Master . . . the *zekr* of the heart consists in the constant presence of the *zekr* in the heart. A *salek* (student) reaches this *zekr* through persistence in his verbal *zekr* . . . the *zekr* of the hidden . . . is hidden within the heart. . . . It is through this *zekr* that the salek becomes the manifestation of the Divine."[8]

Dr. Amineh Pryor discusses Dr. Kianfar's teachings regarding the stages of the *zekr* as follows:

"1. Forget anything other than *zekr*.
2. Settle within the hidden state of being and forget the *zekr*.
3. Settle in the heart, in the hidden heart,

to receive the invitation from the divine. As the Qur'an says, 'Then do you remember me and I will remember you.'"[9]

The various kinds of *zekr* "guide us on our return to the deep harmony of the Divine and the underlying balance of existence."[10]

What is the most important practice for Sufis? Let us next consider the practice of meditation.

# 14

## WHAT IS SUFI MEDITATION?

Recently Dr. Kianfar began his teaching on meditation with a discussion of religion. He explained to his students what religion really is. Religion is a FACT that is within all persons when they are born. He said, you need to discover your religion through practice. In your practice you must collect your energy from its distractions and focus all your energy in your heart. When your energy passes through the eyes of the heart, the FACT becomes truth. When you move out of your body and your physical life into the unseen, hidden realm, you begin the journey of transformation of your self.

Dr. Kianfar said that human beings, from the beginning of time, have had an inner longing for truth — a quest to understand the meaning of life. But the mind has led people to look outside for answers. And religions have become obsessed with the "outside," and with ritual and ceremony. "Wave this green flag and you will go to heaven." Or "Say 'Hallelujah' really loud many times and you will go to heaven." You need to drop all the busyness that has been created under the name of religion.

The mind has also led people to become involved with definitions of words and explanations. Thousands of books have been written, splitting hairs over words and their meanings. This is philosophy; it is not religion.

To find the truth and meaning, you need to return to yourself — your true self. If you look inside, you will find the answers. This will tell you who you really are. You open your spirituality through your practice. To practice is not to talk. Your body and your senses are just tools. You can transform yourself from the physical body to another realm. That is what religion is. Practice opens the door of knowledge and wisdom to the human being. Dr. Kianfar quotes

Amir-al-Moumenin Ali who teaches, "You think you are a small body, but a great universe has been wrapped in you."[1]

Meditation is one of the most important practices on the journey of Sufism. In meditation you will travel to find the source of your being. It is a practice of disconnecting yourself from your limited, physical body and beginning the path of self-transformation to your Divine self. It is a form of prayer; it is a prayer from the heart seeking a connection with God.

Dr. Pryor reports on Dr. Kianfar's teachings in her book, *Sufism: Self, Path and Guide.* She says, "Finding an unchanging point of light and balance is the destination of meditation."[2] Meditation is a path to find truth and to understand the meaning of life. To find that truth and meaning, you need first to find your peaceful center, your true, inner self. You need to approach this search for truth like a scientist in a laboratory. Put all of your energy into it. It will take time and patience. For this search you need solitude and quiet, and that is difficult in this busy world. Set aside a special time and turn off the computer, phone and television. This search for your self will take practice. It is like learning to drive a car.

In her book, *The Psychology of Sufism*, Dr. Pryor says, "The practice of meditation must be taught by a knowledgeable person, by a teacher who has traveled the path of self-knowledge and reached the understanding of unity."[3]

Dr. Kianfar gives directions for meditation. He tells us that we must carefully learn how to meditate and practice with every cell in our body. Begin by holding your intention to become close to God. Discipline yourself and keep your body under control. Sit with your feet on the floor and your back straight, not relaxed. But put no pressure on any part of your head or body. Do not push. Close your eyes, watch your breath and become still.

You will receive temptation from different parts of your body to move. And your mind will become active, thinking about everything and everyone in your life, judging and comparing. It is the nature of the mind to be constantly busy, but this is not helpful to you on this path.

Ignore all these messages. Control your distractions the way you control your car.

Dr. Kianfar says, the first step is to separate yourself from your physical body, including your brain, your mind, your thoughts and your memories. All wishes and desires must be left behind. Let go of your ego; forget even your name. You are searching for your inner self. This is about YOU. Your self is your main concern.

The most important question for you is, how can I get into my heart? The spiritual heart is the source of knowledge. Look in your heart; listen to your heart; focus on your heart.

Collect all of your energy from its scattered places and focus your energy in your heart. Listen for your heart beat. When you find your heart, hold that place through your breathing. Your breathing will purify your system.

Dr. Kianfar explains that at this point you are ready to begin your journey. It begins with a longing for a relationship with God. This is a prayer from the heart, without pronouncing any words. You are trying to move beyond lifetime memories, to remember your being, to find the source of your being. Look for the light. Light makes everything visible and provides guidance for you. Listen for the guidance. Feel the presence of the Divine Source of All Being. Feel yourself surrounded by love. The light is there, but you have to practice to find it. Do this every day and it will transform your life. You will find the secure, stable place inside that does not change.

What you experience is Truth, Reality, Knowledge. This is not knowledge that comes from books or lectures or sermons. This is not about what other people have discovered. This is your own discovery, your own experience, your own knowledge. You are receiving the message from the Source of All Being. This is called a miracle because it is beyond your own power; it is the power of the soul. If you have this experience, you are blessed.[4]

When you experience Truth and Reality, you may find Unity, the oneness of the Universe, God. This is an unchangeable state, one that does not die. Dr. Angha puts it this way: "It is the discovery of the true inner self that must necessarily end in the discovery of one's own essential divinity."[5]

Dr. Angha says that through meditation a person may "gain knowledge that enables one to understand the Divine, the All Knowing, All Embracing, Merciful and Compassionate." She goes on to say "The great expansion of the heart's knowledge will emerge."[6]

Other results of meditation include:

- Your health will improve
- You will find peace, harmony and love
- You will be able to provide peace to society, your community and the world
- You may escape from jealousy, animosity, comparison and judgment
- You will be directed to right action
- You will receive the answers to your questions
- You will discover God's mercy

Meditation and seeking knowledge from the heart is not exclusive to Sufism, although it is called by various other names in other traditions. Cynthia Bourgeault, in *The Heart of Centering Prayer*, says, "contemporary science has taken us far beyond the notion of the heart as a mechanical pump to revision it as 'an electromagnetic generator.'"[7] She also says, "According to the great wisdom traditions of the West (Christian, Jewish, Islamic), the heart is first and foremost an organ of spiritual perception. Its primary function is to . . . see into a deeper reality."[8]

Does the Qur'an provide instruction for prayer and meditation?

# 15

# What Does the Qur'an Say about Prayer?

2:2-3 "This is the Book; in it is guidance sure, without doubt, to those who fear God; who believe in the unseen, are steadfast in prayer..."

2:21 "O ye people! Adore your Guardian-Lord who created you."

2:43 "And be steadfast in prayer; practice regular charity; and bow down your heads with those who bow down."

2:153 "O you who believe! seek help with patient perseverance and prayer."

2:177 "It is righteousness . . . To be steadfast in prayer"

2:238 "Guard strictly your (habit of) prayers, especially the middle prayer; and stand before God In a devout (frame of mind)"

2:256 "Let there be no compulsion in religion."

(Dr. Kianfar explains that there should be nothing forcing you to pray without the approval of your own Divine Essence of knowledge and understanding.)

3:51 "It is God who is my Lord and your Lord; then worship Him. This is a way that is straight."

6:161 "Verily, my Lord Hath guided me to a way that is straight."

7:55 "Call on your Lord with humility and in private."

7:56 "Call on Him in fear and in longing (in your hearts)."

7:180 "The most beautiful names belong to God: So call on Him by them."

10:25 "But God doth call to the home of peace: He doth guide whom He pleaseth to a way that is straight."

11:114 "And establish regular prayers at the two ends of the day and at the approaches of the night; For those things that are good remove those that are evil."

14:40 "O my Lord! Make me one who establishes regular prayer, and also (raise such) among my offspring, O our Lord! And accept Thou my prayer."

17:110 "Say 'Call upon God,' or 'Call upon Rahman': By whatever name ye call upon Him, (it is well): For to Him belong the most beautiful names. Neither speak thy prayer aloud nor speak it in a low tone, but seek a middle course between."

20:14 "Verily, I am God: there is no god but I; so serve thou Me (only), establish regular prayer for celebrating My praise."

22:77 "O ye who believe! Bow down, prostrate yourselves, and adore your Lord; and do good; that ye may prosper."

24:46 "And God guides whom He wills to a way that is straight."

24:56 "So establish regular prayer and give regular charity; and obey the Apostle; that ye may receive mercy."

29:45 "And remembrance of God Is the greatest (thing in life) without doubt."

33:41-42 "O ye who believe! Celebrate the praises of God, and do this often; and glorify Him morning and evening."

62:9 "O ye who believe! When the call is proclaimed to prayer on Friday (the Day of Assembly), hasten earnestly to the remembrance of God."

96:19 "But bow down in adoration, and bring thyself the closer (to God)!"

108:1-2 "To thee have we granted the fount (of abundance). Therefore to thy Lord turn in prayer."[1]

# Part III

Teachers of the Straight Way

# 16

## What Is the Origin of Sufism?

"The origin of Sufism is none other than God Himself," says Dr. Nasr in *The Garden of Truth: The Vision and Promise of Sufism, Islam's Mystical Tradition*. He goes on to say, "This origin must be sought in the word of God, that is, the Qur'an, and in the inner reality of the Prophet, who received this Word and transmitted it to the world."[1]

On the historical plane, Sufism began with the Prophet Mohammed (peace be upon him). He was born in Mecca in what is now Saudi Arabia in approximately 570 C.E. Orphaned at an early age and raised first by his grandfather and then by his uncle, he grew up to become a successful merchant known for his honesty and integrity. When he was forty years old, his life took a dramatic turn. While meditating in a cave on Mount Hira, he was overcome by a visitation from the angel Gabriel. The angel ordered him to "Recite," and "he found the divinely inspired words of a new scripture pouring from his mouth. . . . This holy book would be called the Qur'an."[2]

Dr. Kianfar teaches that the Prophet Mohammed was chosen by God to bring this revelation to mankind. He was a man, not divine, but a messenger of God. He became widely known as a respected spiritual teacher, and he established a new community based on justice and respect for all people. Ultimately, he brought to the world the religion that became known as Islam, founded on the revelations in the Qur'an.

According to one of his biographers, Karen Armstrong, who is not Muslim, Mohammad is "one of the greatest geniuses the world has known. To create a literary masterpiece, to found a major religion and a new world power are not ordinary achievements."[3]

Islam is based on the Rule of Unity, expressed in the statement, repeatedly referred to in this book, *La illa ha illa Allah* (There is nothing except God). The essential quality of Islam is the belief in one God, known as Allah in Arabic, the Almighty, the Eternal, the Source of All Existence.

The word "Islam" means submission or surrender, and while Islam is the name of a religion, it is actually the practice of surrendering one's entire being to the oneness and will of God. Dr. Kianfar says, "One surrenders in order to discover the secret of unity – the unity of the whole of creation and the inner world of self."[4] Today Islam is the second largest religion in the world.

Sufism began on the platform of Mohammad's mosque in Medina. Scholars and wise men from many parts of the world were among those who came to hear Mohammad speak. Following his talks, the scholars gathered on the platform to discuss what they had heard and to inquire more deeply. They became known as *Ahl-e Suffa*, the people of the platform.⁵ These scholars returned to their countries, and Sufism began to spread across the planet. Today Sufism is practiced by more than 65 million people throughout the world.

Sufism is the mystical path of Islam, a beautiful journey into the unseen or inner Reality. It is a way to come to know yourself, a path to discover your pure, inner being. It is a way of exploration for those who want to know: know themselves, where they came from, where they are going – want to know God.⁶

Dr. Kianfar says, "Sufism is the school that opens the door towards understanding and truly knowing God." He continues, Sufism "says that the human mind and the agents of his thoughts cannot understand the essence of God. . . . God must be understood through personal discovery."⁷

Dr. Angha explains, "Sufism's essence – the all surpassing love between the human being and the Divine – has no parallel in the world of surface manifestations, the world of transience." She continues, "Religion to a Sufi is a love affair based on knowledge." The

Sufi journey is often called "the journey of the lovers."[8]

The Sufi's journey may lead to knowledge of the Divine Essence – to God – to the Unity of All Being. This path may lead to the transformation of the body, mind and spirit – of the entire system – to a place of peace, balance, wholeness and stability. Finally, the Sufi may experience the state in which there is no separation between herself and the Divine.

A Sufi student begins this journey under the guidance of a wise and experienced Teacher. The Sufi teacher leads the student to seek self-understanding by opening in her heart through prayer, *zekr* and meditation. It is important to note that the student is never led to follow the Teacher, but the true Teacher leads the student to find her own self.

Here are some things other scholars have said about Sufism.

Dr. Nasr says, "The Prophet of Islam said, 'Whosoever knows his self, knows his Lord;' that is, self-knowledge leads to knowledge of the Divine. Sufism takes this saying very seriously and also puts it into practice."⁹ Dr. Nasr goes on to say, "The Sufi path leads from the desert of outwardness, forgetfulness, selfishness, and falsehood to the Garden of Truth, wherein alone we can realize our true identity and come to know who we are."¹⁰ He also indicates, "Sufism is meant for those who want to wake up, who accept dying to the ego here and now in order to discover the self of all selves and to be consumed in the process in the fire of Divine Love."¹¹

Huston Smith suggests that Sufis want "to encounter God directly in this very lifetime. Now." And they are "willing to assume the heavier disciplines their extravagant goals require."¹²

Martin Lings explains that Sufism is "central, exalted, profound and mysterious" and therefore, sacred. He says, it excludes anything profane.¹³

Frithjof Schuon in *Understanding Islam* says that Sufism is simply the "perfectly sincere" adoration of God.¹⁴

For additional information about Islam and Sufism, see *Principles of Sufism,* by Dr. Nahid Angha.

Who, then, are our holy and wise Teachers who have taught us about Sufism?

# 17

# WHO ARE DR. NAHID ANGHA AND DR. ALI KIANFAR?

Seyyedeh Nahid Angha, Ph. D. is a Sufi scholar, author, lecturer and human-rights activist. She is the co-director and co-founder of the International Association of Sufism (IAS), founder of the International Sufi Women Organization, the executive editor of the journal *Sufism: An Inquiry*, the main representative of the IAS to the United Nations (for Non-Governmental Organizations with the Department of Public Information: NGO/DPI), and the creator of the Building Bridges of Understanding series. She has written over twenty published books and many articles, and has lectured on Sufism, spirituality, human rights and peace at the United Nations, the Smithsonian Institution, the Science and Spirituality forum in Italy, the Council for a Parliament of the World's Religions (CPWR) in South Africa and Spain, the UNESCO's culture of peace conference in Mexico, among others. She was among the distinguished Sufi leaders and scholars invited to gather for the first annual Shakir World Encounters in Marrakesh, Morocco in 2004. She is the first Muslim woman inducted into the Marin Women's Hall of Fame, and honored at Visionary Marin in 2012 by the Marin Interfaith Council. The *Huffington Post* named her as one of the 50 Powerful Women Religious Leaders To Celebrate On International Women's Day, 2014. She has been an active advocate for human rights with a focus on women's rights.

Dr. Angha is the daughter of the 20th century Persian Sufi master Moulana Shah Maghsoud (d. 1980) of the Uwaiysi lineage. Her mother, Mah Talat Etemad Moghadam (d. 2012), was from one of the prominent Persian families, and a descendant of Etemad Saltaneh whose journals and memoirs remain as important manuscripts on the Qajar dynasty of Iran. Her father appointed her to teach and lead Sufi gatherings when she was in her early twenties. She initially held gatherings at her father's khaneghah (Sufi meeting place) in Sufi Abad, Iran, and she continued to teach in the United States. Dr. Angha has studied at the University of Teheran, Iran; SW Missouri State University, United States; and University of Exeter, United Kingdom, and holds doctorate degrees in Psychology and Islamic Studies. Dr. Angha has two daughters and two grandsons and lives in California with her family. She began her humanitarian, inter-religious collaboration and peace efforts in the United States in the early 1980s and continues those efforts today.

Dr. Angha, together with her husband Shah Nazar Seyyed Ali Kianfar, co-founded the International Association of Sufism(IAS), a California non-profit devoted to the teachings of Sufism and Sufi Masters of the past and present (1983). Historically, Sufis have made great contributions to the development of science, literature, poetic styles, astronomy, architectural designs, and more. The IAS has as its mission to make known the interrelations between Sufi principles and scientific principles through lectures, publications, *Sufism An Inquiry Journal*, and creating a forum for a continuing dialogue among Sufis from around the world.

Women have played important roles in the development of art, science, education, entertainment, politics and more, yet the field of religion remains one of the most challenging for women's leadership. It is important to also acknowledge women who, through their endeavors and perseverance, have made contributions towards equality and freedom in the field of religion and spirituality. Dr. Angha has been one of those pioneers whose vision of and works towards humanitarian efforts, inter-religious dialogue and intra-religious movement, equality, peace, and freedom have played fundamental roles in creating the International Sufi Women Organization in 1993.

Her work in collaboration with inter-religious organizations and faith traditions began in the early 1980s. She has served in many faith-based organizations throughout the years, including as a board member as well as a president of the Board of Directors of the Interfaith Center at the Presidio, San Francisco; the Board of Directors of the Marin Interfaith Council; a founding member of the United Religions Initiative (URI) Council for Women; the Board of Directors of Marin Museum of American Indians; a member of the Assembly of the Parliament of the World Religions; a member of the National Interreligious Leadership Delegation; a member of the Assembly for UNESCO: Culture of Peace; a member of the Advisory Board of the Mystic Heart Institute; a member of the Advisory Board of the Institute for World Religions; a Scholar Advisor for Interfaith Sacred Space; and representative at the Goldin Institute.

Dr. Angha has contributed to over one hundred articles ranging from human rights advocacy to translations of the old Sufi texts, poetry, biographies, Islamic philosophy and principles. She is the author and translator of over twenty books including: *A Force Such as the World Has Never Known: Women Creating Change* (co-author, co-editor); *Abdullah Ansari of Hirat (11th century Sufi): One Hundred Stations* (first English translation with commentary); "Abdullah Ansari of Hirat," in *Encyclopedia of Islam* (publishing date 2017); *Ecstasy: The World of Sufi Poetry and Prayers; The Nature of Miracle; A Meditation* (translation); *Principles of Sufism; Psalms of Gods* (translation); *The Journey*.

## Shah Nazar Dr. Seyyed Ali Kianfar

His Holiness Shah Nazar Seyyed Ali Kianfar, Ph.D. is an author, philosopher and a Sufi master, co-founder and co-director of the International Association of Sufism and Editor-in-Chief of *Sufism: An Inquiry*. He is a world-renowned Sufi master who has been teaching spiritual practices and techniques, as well as law, Sufism, and Islamic philosophy, for over forty years. Dr Kianfar was born in Iran.

Dr. Kianfar began his study and devotion to the discipline of Sufism in his twenties under the direct supervision and guidance of 20th century Sufi Master Moulana Shah Maghsoud in the Uwaiysi tarighat (Sufi order). He was later appointed to teach in the Uwaiysi tarighat. Dr. Kianfar was among the first of Moulana Shah Maghsoud's students (numbering in the thousands) to be given this honor. To commemorate the significance, Moulana Shah Maghsoud gave Dr. Kianfar the honorary title Shah Nazar (The Sight of the King). Moulana Shah Maghsoud and Dr. Kianfar had a close relationship and Moulana Shah Maghsoud considered Dr. Kianfar his spiritual son. Dr. Kianfar began his teaching in Iran and continues to teach throughout North America, Europe, and the Middle East.

Dr. Kianfar has given lectures and taught classes internationally on "Love & Wisdom", the Bible, Qur'an and the Hadith. This includes speaking engagements at the United Nations, UNESCO, the University of California, Berkeley, Dominican University, Stanford University, the California Institute of Integral Studies, and the United Religions Initiative.

He is actively involved in international interfaith initiatives to help raise awareness about the peaceful dimensions of religion and spirituality and to open the lines of communication for a better understanding of humanity.

Dr. Kianfar, together with his wife Seyyedeh Dr. Nahid Angha, launched the "Sufism Symposium" in 1983, which was the first time in the history of Sufism that Sufi masters from all around the world and from different tarighats came together with each other and leaders of other religions, scientists, poets, and spiritual musicians. The symposium has become a successful annual event held in different locations throughout the world.

The practical spiritual techniques Dr. Kianfar uses are based on the ancient wisdom of the prophets and have been used by spiritual masters throughout the ages. It is the first time in history that the introduction to and preparation for *chelleh* (40 days duration of purification) have been offered publicly. It is also the first time that the highly spiritual practice of purification has been combined with psychological training.

His books include *Illumination of the Names: Meditation by Sufi Masters on the Ninety-Nine Beautiful Names of God*, *Seasons of the Soul*, *The Zekr*, *Fatimah* (in Farsi), *History of the Robe*, and *An Introduction to Religion*. In addition, Seyyed Dr. Ali Kianfar publishes regularly in *Sufism: An Inquiry*.

# 18

# What Is the International Association of Sufism?

The International Association of Sufism (IAS) is a non-profit, humanitarian organization headquartered in Novato, California, and a Non-Governmental Organization (NGO) of the United Nations, Department of Public Information. IAS was founded in 1983 by Dr. Nahid Angha and Dr. Ali Kianfar who have served since then as Co-Directors.

IAS provides a global forum for continuing dialogue among Sufis, scholars, interfaith leaders, poets and artists from diverse cultures and Sufi schools and from numerous countries around the world. IAS provides humanitarian service to people in need in many countries and is an advocate for human rights and especially women's rights. The Directors and members have participated in and made presentation to the Parliament of the World's Religions, United Religions Initiative, the Institute for World Religions, and the National Interreligious Leadership. In 2000 IAS was awarded UNESCO's "Messenger of Peace" award.

The IAS is also an Islamic Sufi school with approximately 85 students from throughout the San Francisco Bay Area with many more across the country and around the world. The school has members from a variety of races and ethnic backgrounds. The group holds regular gatherings and *Zekr* prayer services at the Khanaghah in Novato. Another chapter of the school is located in Seattle, Washington. Students receive instruction and training from Holy Teachers Dr. Nahid Angha and Dr. Ali Kianfar. Dr. Angha is descended from a long lineage of Sufi teachers, and both she and Dr. Kianfar were designated as teachers by one of the 20th century's great Sufi Masters, Moulana Shah Maghsoud Sadegh Angha. The Holy Teachers receive no monetary compensation for their spiritual work.

In 1988 Dr. Angha and Dr. Kianfar began the journal *Sufism: An Inquiry*, the first journal dedicated to Sufism published in the US and distributed internationally. In 1993, Dr. Angha founded the first international *Sufi Women Organization* (SWO) to support, advocate, and educate for human rights with focus on women's rights, and especially Muslim women's rights. SWO has presented interfaith and Sufism conferences and retreats for women, as well as lecture series since its inception.

For the past 24 years, the IAS has brought together faith leaders and scholars from around the world to share wisdom and advance peace and human rights through the annual Sufism Symposium, an international, multicultural conference, and the *"Songs of the Soul" Festival of Poetry and Sacred Music*. Symposia have been held in the several parts of the U.S., and in Scotland, Egypt and Spain.

Other IAS programs and activities include:

*Forty Days: Alchemy of Tranquility Program*
This program integrates western psychological principles with Sufi mysticism for an innovative psychotherapeutic approach. Day long and weekend retreats provide experiential learning for participants.

*Building Bridges of Understanding*
This educational program for the community is presented in conjunction with the Humanities Department of Dominican University of California in San Rafael. For 15 years these programs have introduced the public to the wisdom teachings of various religions and examined current social issues.

*Institute for Sufi Studies*
The Institute provides classes and workshops open to the public based on Sufism, the Qur'an, and the wisdom of other holy books, as well as programs on meditation.

*Community Healing Centers*
Bay area counseling centers provide individual and group psychotherapy combining Sufi healing practices with Western psychology.

*Voices for Justice*
Youth leaders advocate for children's rights through educational programs, events and community service, including coordination with UNICEF.

*The Prison Project*
Sufi students contribute books, teach meditation and encourage positive change in inmates in Bay Area prisons and jails, and carry on correspondence with inmates across the US.

*Taneen, Sufi Music Ensemble*
Sufi musicians compose and perform music inspired by Sufi poetry and the Qur'an on western and eastern instruments. They have issued a number of recordings and have performed in several countries around the world.

*Avay-i-Janaan "Echoes of the Unseen"*
This international group of poets, visual artists and musicians weave together science and mystical tradition to express the connection between the self and the universe.

# Endnotes

**CHAPTER ONE: HAVE HUMAN BEINGS ALWAYS PRAYED?**

1. *Inspirations on the Holy Qur'an,* Introduction by Shah Nazar Seyyed Ali Kianfar, p. 23
2. Thich Nhat Hahn, *The Energy of Prayer,* Introduction by Larry Dossey, M.D., p. 9
3. Donald Spoto, *In Silence: Why We Pray,* p. 5
4. https://sourcebooks.fordham.edu/ancient/1600babylonianprayers.asp
5. Spoto, p. 5
6. https://www.newworldencyclopedia.org/entry/Lascaux
7. https://www.Britannica.com/topic/prayer/forms-of-prayer-in-the-religions-of-the-world
8. Timothy Verdon, *Art and Prayer,* p. v
9. Philip and Carol Zaleski, *Prayer: A History,* p. 31
10. Ibid., quoting Sigmund Freud, pp. 26-27
11. Ibid., p. 28

[12] https://www.pewresearch.org/fact-tank/2016/05/04/5-facts-about-prayer

[13] Larry Dossey, M.D., *Prayer is Good Medicine,* p. 60

[14] Amineh Amelia Pryor, *Sufism: Self, Path and Guide*, pp. 45-47

## CHAPTER TWO: WHAT IS PRAYER?

[1] Sarah Hastings Mullin, *The Book of Self*, quoting Ali Kianfar, p. 75

[2] Coleman Barks and Michael Green, *The Illuminated Prayer,* p. 26

[3] Pryor, *Sufism,* p. 149

[4] Spoto, p. xiv

[5] Sherry Ruth Anderson and Patricia Hopkins, *The Feminine Face of God.* p. 131 and p. 146

[6] Larry Dossey, M.D., *Healing Words*, p. 6

[7] Brother David Steindl-Rast, *Gratefulness, the Heart of Prayer,* p. 39

[8] Richard Rohr, Daily Meditation from the Center for Action and Contemplation, February 7, 2017

[9] Dossey, *Healing Words,* p. 209

10 *Inspirations on the Holy Qur'an*, Introduction by Ali Kianfar, p. 22
11 Robert Llewellyn, *The Joy of Saints,* quoting Isaac of Syria, p. 31
12 Seyyed Hossein Nasr, *The Garden of Truth*, p. 101
13 Spoto, p. xix
14 Barks and Green, p. 70
15 Llewellyn, p. 190
16 Spoto, quoting R. W. Maqsood, p. 36
17 Ibid., p. 142

**CHAPTER THREE: WHAT ARE THE DIFFERENT TYPES OF PRAYER?**
1 William C. Chittick, *Sufism: A Beginner's Guide*, p. 64
2 Verdon, p. 147
3 Anne Lamott, *Help, Thanks, Wow,* p. 56, p. 65, p. 49
4 Nasr, *Garden*, p. 100
5 Llewellyn, p. 225
6 Dossey, *Healing Words*, p. 24
7 Larry Dossey, M.D., *Prayer is Good Medicine, p. 59*

8 Nahid Angha, oral teaching
9 *Principles of Sufism,* p. 81
10 Philip and Carol Zaleski, p. 197
11 Cynthia Bourgeault, *The Heart of Centering Prayer*, p. 13
12 Ibid., p. 126
13 Anderson and Hopkins, p. 139
14 https://www.buddhagroove.com/prayer-wheels
15 Philip and Carol Zaleski, p. 4
16 Dossey, *Healing Words,* p. 71
17 Philip and Carol Zaleski, p. 329
18 Ibid., p. 83
19 Pamela Brode, *The Power of Prayer,* p.2
20 Nahid Angha, *Principles*, p. 49

**CHAPTER FOUR: WHY DO WE PRAY?**

1 Nahid Angha, "When We Need More Prayers," *Sufism: An Inquiry,* Vol. IX, No. 4, p.4
2 Nahid Angha, *The Journey: Seyr va Soluk*, p. 7 and p. 9
3 Nahid Angha, *Principles,* p. 81
4 Rohr, Daily Meditation, September 16, 2018

5. Philip and Carol Zaleski, p. 99
6. Anderson and Hopkins, p. 125
7. Lamott, quoting C. S. Lewis, p. 100
8. Ali Kianfar, *The Zekr*, p. 16
9. Nahid Angha, *Principles*, p. 83
10. Sarah Hastings Mullin, *The Book of Self*, p. 61
11. *Inspirations*, chapter by Sarah Hastings Mullin, p. 121
12. Nahid Angha, *Principles*, quoting Sheikh Kazerouni, p.88

### CHAPTER FIVE: TO WHOM DO WE PRAY?
1. Nahid Angha, oral teaching
2. *Ali Kianfar, oral teaching*
3. Martin Lings, *What Is Sufism?* P. 49
4. Anderson and Hopkins, p. 125
5. Lamott, p. 6
6. Ali Kianfar, *An Introduction to Religion*, pp. 43-44

### CHAPTER SIX: WHAT ARE THE RESULTS OF PRAYER?
1. *Inspirations*, chapter by Katherine Preston, p. 142

2. Llewellyn Vaughan-Lee, *Prayer of the Heart*, p. 61
3. Nahid Angha, *Principles*, pp. 82-83
4. Hammerle, Arife Ellen; Newman, Safa Ali Michael; Pryor, Amineh Amelia, *Sufi Grace*, chapter by Pryor, p. 99
5. Nahid Angha, *The Nature of Miracle*, pp. 10-11
6. Ali Kianfar, oral teaching
7. Anderson and Hopkins, p. 133
8. Ibid., p. 139, quoting Maya Angelou
9. Hahn, p. 13 and p. 39

**CHAPTER SEVEN: WHAT HAVE SCIENTIFIC STUDIES REVEALED ABOUT PRAYER?**

1. Dossey, *Prayer*, p. 14
2. Ibid., pp. 2-3
3. Ibid., p. 49 and p. 66-67
4. Dossey, *Healing*, p. 97
5. Dossey, *Prayer*, p. 129
6. Philip and Carol Zaleski, p. 343
7. Ibid., p. 343 and p. 346
8. Dossey, *Healing*, pp. 179-185
9. Ibid., p. 44 and p. 52
10. Philip and Carol Zaleski, p. 346

## Chapter Eight: What Are Some Beautiful Prayers?

1. Mah Talat Etemad Moghadam Angha, *Al-Momenon: The Faithful*, p. 180
2. Moulana Shah Maghsoud (Sadegh Angha), *A Meditation: Payam-e-del*, pp. 2-4
3. Seyyedeh Hamaseh Angha Kianfar, unpublished manuscript
4. Lings, p. 11
5. https://www.jewfaq.org/shemaref.htm
6. *The Holy Bible*, King James version, Psalms 23: 1-6
7. Ibid., Matthew 6: 9-13
8. https://www.Catholicplanet.com/catholic/hail.htm, based on Luke 1:28-35, 42-48
9. *The Book of Common Prayer*, p. 833
10. Ibid., p. 134
11. Philip and Carol Zaleski, pp. 139-142
12. Ibid., p. 126
13. *The Book of Common Prayer*, p. 815
14. *Bhagavagita*, translated with notes by Radhakrishnan, p. 299, quoting from Mahatma Gandhi, *Songs from Prison*, p.52
15. Rabindranath Tagore, *Gitanjali*, p. 13

## Chapter Ten: How Do Sufis Prepare Pray?

1. Ali Kianfar, *The Zekr*, p. 4
2. Ibid., p. 12
3. Ibid., p. 12
4. Ibid., p. 12
5. Ibid., p. 13
6. *Unveiling Islam*, p. 9
7. Ali Kianfar, *The Zekr*, p. 14
8. Ibid., p. 19

## Chapter Eleven: What Is *Salat* – The Sufi Daily Prayer?

1. Desmond Steward, *Mecca*, p. 17
2. Ibid., from dust jacket, front flap
3. Hammerle, Newman, Pryor, p. 155
4. Nasr, *Garden*, pp. 16-18
5. Ali Kianfar, *The Zekr*, pp. 16-17
6. Mullin, p. 6
7. *Inspirations*, chapter by Sherri Brown, p. 62
8. Nasr, *Garden*, p. 100
9. Barks and Green, *The Illuminated Prayer*, p. 34

**CHAPTER TWELVE: WHAT IS THE SUFI PRAYER CALLED THE FATIHA?**

1. https:www.sufism.org/al-fatiha, translated by Kabir Helminski
2. Ali Kianfar, *The Zekr*, p. 21
3. Nasr, *The Heart of Islam: Enduring Values for Humanity*, p. 131
4. Frithjof Schuon, *Understanding Islam*, p. 67
5. Mullin, pp. 37-39
6. Ibid, pp. 55-58
7. Annemarie Schimmel, *Islam: An Introduction*, p. 48

**CHAPTER THIRTEEN: WHAT IS *ZEKR* – THE SUFI PRAYER OF REMEMBRANCE?**

1. Nahid Angha, *Principles*, p. 84
2. *Inspirations,* chapter by Sheikh Said Hassan, p. 89
3. Ibid., Introduction by Ali Kianfar, p. 12
4. Ibid., chapter by Amelia Amineh Pryor, p. 184
5. Ibid., Introduction by Ali Kianfar, p. 12
6. Ibid., Introduction by Ali Kianfar, p. 12
7. Ibid., Introduction by Ali Kianfar, p. 11-12
8. Nahid Angha, *Principles*, p. 82

[9] *Inspirations*, chapter by Pryor, p. 180
[10] Hammerle, Newman, Pryor, chapter by Pryor, p. 93
[11] Ibid., chapter by Pryor, p. 99

### CHAPTER FOURTEEN: WHAT IS SUFI MEDITATION?

[1] Ali Kianfar, oral teaching
[2] Pryor, *Sufism*, p. 131
[3] Amineh Amelia Pryor, *The Psychology of Sufism*, p. 40
[4] Ali Kianfar, oral teaching
[5] Nahid Angha, *The Journey*, p. 8
[6] Nahid Angha, *Sufi Wisdom*, pp. 53-54
[7] Cynthia Bourgeault, *The Heart of Centering Prayer*, p. 60
[8] Ibid., p. 54

### CHAPTER FIFTEEN: WHAT DOES THE QUR'AN SAY ABOUT PRAYER?

[1] These quotations are from Abdullah Yusuf Ali, *The Holy Qur'an*, English translation

### CHAPTER SIXTEEN: WHAT IS THE ORIGIN OF SUFISM?

[1] Nasr, *Garden*, p. 166

2 Armstrong, *Muhammad*, p. 45
3 Ibid., p. 52
4 *Inspirations,* Introduction by Ali Kianfar, p. 29
5 Hammerle, Newman, Pryor, p. xi
6 Haymaker, *The Light of the Heart*, p. 2
7 Shah Nazar Ali Kianfar, *An Introduction to Religion*, pp. 47-48
8 Nahid Angha, *Sufism: The Journey of the Lovers*, p. 5 and p. 8
9 Nasr, *Garden*, p. 5
10 Ibid., p. 6
11 Ibid., p. 22
12 Huston Smith, *The World's Religions*, p. 259
13 Lings, p. 92
14 Schuon, p. 187

# BIBLIOGRAPHY

Agnes, Michael, editor, *Webster's New World Dictionary and Thesaurus,* Second Edition (New York, Hungry Minds, Inc.) 2002

Ali, Abdullah Yusuf, *The Holy Qur'an,* English translation (Elmhurst, NY, Tahrike Tarsile Qur'an, Inc.) 1987

Anderson, Sherry Ruth, and Hopkins, Patricia, *The Feminine Face of God: The Unfolding of the Sacred in Women* (New York, Bantam Books) 1991

Angha, Hazrat Mir Ghotbeddin Mohammad, *Destination Eternity,* translated by Nahid Angha (San Rafael, CA, International Association of Sufism) 1997

Angha, Mah Talat Etemad-Moghadam, *Al-Momenon: The Faithful,* translated by Nahid Angha (San Rafael, CA, International Association of Sufism) 2000

Angha, Nahid, *Ecstasy: The World of Sufi Poetry and Prayer* (San Rafael, CA, International Association of Sufism) 1998
——, *The Journey: Seyr va Soluk* (San Rafael, CA, International Association of Sufism) 1996
——, *The Nature of Miracle* (San Rafael, CA, International Association of Sufism) 1993
——, *Principles of Sufism* (Fremont, CA, Asian Humanities Press) 1991
——, *Sufi Wisdom: The Collected Words of Sufi Master Nahid Angha,* (San Rafael, CA, International Association of Sufism) 2016
——, *Sufism: The Journey of the Lovers* (San Rafael, CA, International Association of Sufism) 1998
——, "When We Need More Prayers," *Sufism: An Inquiry*, Vol. IX, No. 4, 2001
Angha, Nahid, et al., *Sufi Women: The Journey towards the Beloved* (San Rafael, CA, International Association of Sufism) 1998
Armstrong, Karen, *Islam: A Short History* (New York, Random House) 2002
——, *Muhammad: A Biography of the Prophet* (New York, Harper Collins) 1992

Arshed, Aneela Khalid, *The Bounty of Allah* (New York, The Crossroads Publishing Co.) 1999

Barks, Coleman and Green, Michael, *The Illuminated Prayer* (New York, Ballantine Books) 2000

*Bhagavadgita*, translated with notes by Radhakrishnan (Bombay, India, George Allen & Unwin) 1971

*The Book of Common Prayer and Administration of the Sacraments and Other Rites and Ceremonies of the Church Together with the Psalter or Psalms of David According to the use of The Episcopal Church* (New York, Church Publishing Inc.) 1979

Bourgeault, Cynthia. *The Heart of Centering Prayer: Nondual Christianity in Theory and Practice*, (Boulder, CO, Shambhala Publications) 2016

Brode, Pamela, *The Power of Prayer* (Wilmette, IL, Baha'i Publishing) 2006

*Caravan: Biographies from the Sufism Symposium 1994 – 2014* (San Rafael, CA, International Association of Sufism) 2015

Chittick, William C., *Sufism: A Beginner's Guide* (Oxford, UK, Oneworld Publications) 2008

*Deliverance: Words from the Prophet Mohammad,* translated by Nahid Angha (San Rafael, CA, International Association of Sufism) 1995

Dossey, Larry, *Healing Words: The Power of Prayer and the Practice of Medicine* (San Francisco, Harper Collins) 1993

———, *Prayer Is Good Medicine: How to Reap the Healing Benefits of Prayer* (San Francisco, Harper Collins) 1996

Edson, John Hank, *Radical Equality: Overcoming America's Spiritual Crisis* (San Francisco, Democracy Press) 2009

*Gates of Repentance: The New Union Prayerbook for the Days of Awe* (New York, Central Conference of American Rabbis) 1996

Hanh, Thich Nhat, *The Energy of Prayer: How to Deepen Your Spiritual Practice* (Berkeley, Parallax Press) 2006

Hammerle, Arife Ellen, *The Sacred Journey:*

*Unfolding Self Essence* (San Rafael, CA, International Association of Sufism) 2000
———, *Reflections* (San Rafael, CA, International Association of Sufism) 2018
Hammerle, Arife Ellen; Newman, Safa Ali Michael; Pryor, Amineh Amelia, *Sufi Grace* (Bloomington, IN, Author House) 2009
Harvey, Andrew and Anne Baring, *The Divine Feminine* (Berkeley, CA, Conari Press) 1996
Haymaker, Halima JoAnn, *The Light of the Heart* (San Rafael, CA, International Association of Sufism) 2017
*Holy Bible,* King James Version (New York, The World Publishing Company) undated
*Holy Bible,* Revised Standard Version (New York, Thomas Nelson & Sons) 1952
https://www.Britannica.com/topic/prayer/forms-of-prayer-in-the-religions-of-the-world
https://www.buddhagroove.com/prayer-wheels
https://www.catholicplanet.com/catholic/hail.htm
https://www.jewfaq.org/shemaref.htm

https://www.newwworldencyclopedia.org/entry/Lascaux
https://www.pewresearch.org/fact-tank/2016/05/04/5-facts-about-prayer
https://sourcebooks.fordham.edu/ancient/1600Babylonianprayers.asp
https://www.sufism.org/al-fatiha
*Inspirations on the Holy Qur'an, A Collection of Essays with an introduction by Ali Kianfar* (San Rafael, CA, International Association of Sufism) 2013
Kianfar, Seyyedeh Hamaseh Angha, unpublished manuscript
Kianfar, Shah Nazar Ali, *Illumination of the Names* (San Rafael, CA, International Association of Sufism) 2011
———, *An Introduction to Religion* (San Rafael, CA, International Association of Sufism) 1996
———, *Seasons of the Soul* (San Rafael, CA, International Association of Sufism) 2006
———, *The Zekr* (San Rafael, CA, International Association of Sufism) 1985
Kianfar, Shah Nazar Ali, et al., *Human*

*Self, Volume I: Body* (San Rafael, CA, International Association of Sufism) 2013

Ladinsky, Daniel, *I Heard God Laughing* (New York, Penguin Group (USA), Inc.) 2006

———, *Love Poems from God* (New York, Penguin Group (USA), Inc.) 2002

Lamott, Anne, *Help, Thanks, Wow: The Three Essential Prayers* (New York, Riverhead Books) 2012

Lings, Martin, *What Is Sufism?* (Cambridge, UK, The Islamic Texts Society) 1993

Link, Mark, SJ, *You: Prayer for Beginners and Those Who Have Forgotten How* (Allen, TX, Argus Communications) 1976

Lippman, Thomas, *Understanding Islam: An Introduction to the Muslim World* (New York, Penguin Books) 1990

Llewellyn, Robert, *The Joy of Saints* (Springfield, IL, Templegate Publishers) 1989

Maghsoud, Moulana Shah, *Manifestations of Thought,* translated by Nahid Angha (San Rafael, CA, ETRI Publications) 1980

———, *A Meditation: Payam-e-del*, translated

by Nahid Angha (San Rafael, CA, International Association of Sufism) 1994

———, *Psalms of Gods,* translated by Nahid Angha (San Rafael, CA, International Association of Sufism) 1991

Mullin, Sarah Hastings, *The Book of Self* (San Rafael, CA, International Association of Sufism) 2015

Nasr, Seyyed Hossein, *The Garden of Truth: The Vision and Promise of Sufism, Islam's Mystical Tradition* (New York, NY, Harper Collins) 2007

———, *The Heart of Islam: Enduring Values for Humanity* (San Francisco, Harper Collins) 2002

Newman, Michael Brill, *The Gift of the Robe* (San Rafael, CA, International Association of Sufism) 2000

Ozelsel, Michaela, *Forty Days: A Diary of a Traditional Solitary Sufi Retreat* (Brattleboro, VT, Threshold Books,) 1996

Pryor, Amineh Amelia, *Psychology in Sufism* (San Rafael, CA, International Association of Sufism) 2000

———, *Sufism: Self, Path and Guide* (San Rafael, CA, International Association of Sufism) 2017

Rohr, Richard, Daily Meditation from the Center for Action and Contemplation, https://cac.org February 7, 2018; September 16, 2018

———, *What Do We Do with the Bible* (Albuquerque, NM, CAC Publishing) 2018

Schimmel, Annemarie, *Islam: An Introduction* (Albany, NY, State University of New York) 1992

Schuon, Frithjof, *Understanding Islam* (Bloomington, IN, World Wisdom Books, Inc.) 1994

Shah, Indris, *The Sufis* (Garden City, NY, Doubleday & Company, Inc.) 1971

Siddiqui, Haroon, *Being Muslim* (Toronto, ON, Canada, Groundwood Books) 2008

Smith, Huston, *The World's Religions* (New York, NY, Harper Collins) 1991

Spoto, Donald, *In Silence: Why We Pray* (New York, NY, Viking Compass) 2004

*Stations of the Sufi Path*, The One Hundred

*Fields (Sad Maydan) of Abdullah Ansari of Herat*, translated and introduction by Nahid Angha (Cambridge, UK, Archetype) 2010

Steindl-Rast, Brother David *Gratefulness, the Heart of Prayer* (Ramsey, NJ, Paulist Press) 1984

Stewart, Desmond, *Mecca* (New York, Newsweek Books) 1980

Suhrawardi, Shahabuddin, *The Awarif-ul-Ma'Arif* (Delhi, India, Taj Co.) 2011

Talib, Imam Ali ibn Abu, *Peak of Eloquence* (Elmhurst, NY, Tahrike Tarsile Qur'an, Inc.) 1996

Tagore, Rabindranath, *Gitanjali* (Mineola, NY, Dover Publications) 2000

*Unveiling Islam: An Introduction to Fundamental Beliefs,* a pamphlet from the Institute for Sufi Studies (San Rafael, International Association of Sufism) 2001

Vaughan-Lee, Llewellyn, *Prayer of the Heart* (Point Reyes, CA, The Golden Sufi Center) 2017

Verdon, Timothy, *Art and Prayer* (Brewster, MA, Paraclete Press) 2014

Wilber, Ken, *Integral Spirituality* (Boston, Integral Books) 2006

www.catholicplanet.com/catholic/hail.htm

www.jewfaq.org/shemaref.htm

www.newwworldencyclopedia.org/entry/Lascaux

www.pewresearch.org/fact-tank/2016/05/04/5-facts-about-prayer

www.sufism.org/al-fatiha

Zaleski, Philip and Carol, *Prayer: A History* (New York, NY, Houghton Mifflin Co.) 2005

# Acknowledgements

Dr. Nahid Angha and Dr. Ali Kianfar have given me the greatest gift of all by accepting me as their student. *Alhamdulallah.* They have provided the wisdom, teachings and guidance that have made this book possible. To them I am deeply grateful. I wish to acknowledge and thank The Reverend Deacon Marcia Tyriver for the opportunity to participate in the interfaith Contemplative Prayer Group at Saint Patrick's Episcopal Church in Kenwood, California, in which we have explored some of these thoughts, and for her additions to this book. Sufi Sheikh Jamal Granick, Methodist minister The Reverend Betty Pagett, Presbyterian Anne Senf, and Buddhist Susan Carney, all contributed personal experiences, understanding and prayers that have been incorporated in the text. Zen Buddhist Priest Eko-Sana

Ray Estebrook honored me by talking with me about his practice, on his death bed, just weeks before he peacefully left his body. The members of the Taneen Sufi Music Ensemble, Sheikh Salman Baruti, Dr. Soraya Clow, Sheikh Salim Matchette, Salima Patton Matchette, and Taher Roybal, contributed the manuscript for words to Sufi *zekr* introduced to them by Dr. Angha. Thanks also to Sharon von Haesler who read and corrected an early version of this book and to Sheikh Salim Matchette for reading the final version. No one has spent more time and careful study, editing and improving various versions of this manuscript, than my Sufi sister Dr. Amineh Amelia Pryor. To her I am thankful beyond words. With gratitude to Dr. Matthew Davis of BEAR INTERNATIONAL PremiereGraphicDesignInstitute for the cover design. Above all, thanks to my husband, Will Haymaker, for his years of devotion and love and for praying with me in the sanctuary that we have made of our home.

*"He doth guide whom he pleaseth to a Way that is straight."*
*Holy Qur'an 10:25*

www.ingramcontent.com/pod-product-compliance
Lightning Source LLC
Chambersburg PA
CBHW060751050426
42449CB00008B/1362